Chris Sibia

A Product of My Environment

London's Finest Distribution

London, UK

London's Finest Distribution

Copyright © 2016 by Christopher Aransibia

The right of Christopher Aransibia to be identified as the Author
of the Work has been asserted by him in accordance with the
Copyright, Designs and Patents Act 1988.

First published in Great Britain in 2016
by LONDON'S FINEST DISTRIBUTION

Disclaimer
This is a work of creative nonfiction. The events are portrayed to the best of my
memory. While all the stories in this book are true, some names and identifying
details have been changed to protect the privacy of the people involved.

ISBN 978-0-9935900-0-9

Printed and bound by
CPI Group (UK) Ltd, Croydon, CR0 4YY

Elaine,
Thank you for your support.
Enjoy! Sibs xxx

This is written in Jamaican and English
street language idiom.

A Product of My Environment

PRAISE FOR
A Product of My Environment

"Chris Sibia shows his unadulterated bravery by baring his inner soul and shortcomings in part one of his autobiography, which drew many parallels with my life growing up on the opposite end of London. The story made me cringe, laugh but overall entertained." **- VON MOZAR: AUTHOR**

AUTHOR'S ACKNOWLEDGEMENTS

Well what can I say; this is a greatly anticipated milestone in a very long journey for me. At some points I thought I wouldn't make it, but I have. Here now looking at a completed part one, I have to say it's all been worth it. I believe we all have at least one book in us, but if not for the events in my life that made me decide to write this book, I would have kept my life story to myself to smile on reflection from time to time at my own convenience.

I thought carefully about my target audience and my intensions for writing this book. This is the reason I decided to write with Jamaican idioms. I must also say, I'm no English literature academic in any sense of the word so please don't judge me on that. I've written this book how I speak. I'm a road man who decided later on in life to educate myself and inspire others as I realise knowledge will set us free.

A wise man once said, "It's time for us man to start telling our story from our mouth." That's the truth! If we don't, do we have the right to be upset with any others representation of us?

Mummy, I have to start my thanks with you. I wouldn't be here without you. At the age you were when you decided to have me, you could have easily kept me as a 'what if' in your universal consciousness. Then, for all those years, the stress I caused you with my lifestyle. The admiration and love I have for you, I can't verbalize. I have been concerned for years now with how I would repay you for all you have done. But realize, you have done so much for me, I might never. Books and reading is something you always encouraged, so even though this book isn't written for you. This book is for you Mummy. I hope to make you proud of me one day!

Dad, you're my dad and I love you for that but I've written this book about my life and we both know what part you played in that.

Bruv, you being the older that you were cushioned me as a yute growing on the endz. Thank you, it was the love you had on road that was extended to me. I do feel like you abandoned me at a critical stage in my life but it's alright, I realized as I got older, you needed a big brother so don't watch nothing.

Banks, I'm greatly indebted to you my brother. I wouldn't even have started this book if it wasn't for you. I probably still wouldn't be able to read.

Noel, I changed your name in this book but if you ever do read it, you will know who you are in it. Good friends are hard to find, I'm sorry for what happened. You helped me more than you know so you have to get a mention here now.

Pauly, your energy, finesse, style and determination can be a lesson to us all. You kept me motivated without even knowing it time and time again. Family, you nice! Keep doing what you do.

Links Man, you've been around for most of the life I remember and you still around. My dawg for life!

Dan, Sim and John, right now a rest in peace message goes out to Aunt and Uncle. We gonna make it, remember I told you.

Steveo, thank you for everything over the years! Your another role model for the world. Let the world see you shine brother.

Marky, you were the older brother I wished I had along

with Reggie, Edd's and the rest of my olders. Respect is due so it's duly given

Sheriff, road was never the same for me after I linked you. Those were the days!

Courts, you don't know how you helped me with that little situation. I might have ended up in a mess. Big up fam!

Tucked Up, you dun know we HOT2DEATH for life.

Tony D, you still one of the best I've heard. I hope you get the recognition you deserve.

Schelle, an extra special thanks goes out to you. You're the reason this book is in print today. When I asked you to help me with it, I know it was a mess. A lot of editors had looked at it before you, seen the word count and the work that needed to be done and run for the hills. You sat down, night after night arranging and rearranging until it started to look like a book. Blessings from the most high be with you always.

Johnny J, I finally meet you on the other side. Hold it up always, remember slipping ain't allowed.

I also want to thank all the other English urban authors that came before me, one inspiring the next. I'm not saying I wouldn't still be here but I might not have had the opportunity to meet Von Mozar. Von, your experience as a writer, your passion for your art and your work ethic was an inspiration to me and it continues to be. Your commitment to seeing a project through to the end should be adopted by all. Let's put UK urban literature on the map where it's supposed to be.

There are a lot of extra people I haven't mentioned here that have also helped me a lot in the final stages of bringing this part 1 to print. I would like to say a big thank you to you all, you know who you are.

I also have to take this opportunity to thank Cup Cake Brown. A Piece of Cake was the book that made me believe I could write my own. A must read for inspiration in the face of adversity. If she can do it we all can.

Ishmahil, your advice to put some meat on the bones as you put it was painful at the time but true. After six plus years with edit upon edit behind me, I didn't want to hear that and if I didn't respect your greater consciousness and deep down understand your criticism I wouldn't have listened. Keep speaking up my brother, you do that well.

And now I come to Kayan, the reason I wrote this book. My little solider! You made Mummy and Daddy proud and this is for you in loving memory. Rest in peace Son! A loving appreciation also goes to his mum, without you there wouldn't have been that spark. No chain of events that brings me here today. Thank You!

PROLOGUE

YEAR 1984

CHAPTER I

I don't remember much before the age of six, but that all changed on a summer trip to Barbados, just before my seventh birthday. The blazing sun, palm trees and sandy beaches were definitely unforgettable, but I remember Barbados for other reasons.

I remembered ramping (playing) in Grandma's front garden, I was throwing rocks up into the palm trees at the Monkeys, when I heard faint screams in the distance. Tru it sounded like it was coming from Grandma's back yard. I went to see wha gwan (what was going on) and that's when I found her. Grandma, there in this pit, cockroaches crawling all over her, a funny feeling went straight to my stomach as I opened my mouth in shock. 'Grandma!' Panic set in as I screamed and realised she could drown in there. *I loved my grandma.* I went and called Mumsy and Uncle and we got her out. I looked at her as she watched me, out of breath, looking bedraggled and flustered and wondered how the fuck she ended up in that pit screaming for help.

That summer was crazy for a little man like me, between one cousin's little Chihuahua biting my foot for no reason and another cousin letting me drive his wife's car. The car was a little automatic and when he see me watching him drive, it's like he read my mind. I was thinking. *It's like a big bumper car I can't bump*. Even though, I had never driven a bumper car, in my mind I thought I could. He loved a drink, my cousin did, a proper *alki* he was. And he was fat and lazy too, so that didn't help. We were about five minutes from his yard when, out of nowhere, he asked; 'Hey Chris, you want to drive?' Without me even answering, he said, 'Swap seats.'

I said, 'You serious?'

'Yeah!' he said.

I was on it! I jumped in the drivers' seat and started driving. I'm driving down this hill all now? The scenery was beautiful and I'm feeling real, I'm actually driving. He hadn't even told me what pedal the brake was, but I was going on with tings (doing good) until I needed to make a right turn. As I turned, I realised I was going to hit a fence. Panicking, I kept turning. I totally missed the fence, but now I'm heading for a tree. It was all too much. I totally forgot the brake, hit this tree and fucked up his wife's car.

No one blamed me but that didn't stop me blaming myself. I left Barbados to go home back to London feeling guilty.

That's where life started for me.

DRASTIC CHANGES

CHAPTER ONE

Fuck me that shit hurts! I remember thinking as my brother hit me with a rock he threw at me. Blood stained my favourite blue T shirt as I lifted my arm trying to make sure the blood didn't stain my jeans too. It was dripping fast and starting to sting. We were playing 'Let's see who gets fucked up first' out on Higham Hill, the main road about five minutes walk from home. Tru I loved being with him, it didn't matter what we were doing; whatever he was playing I was trying to play too. I thought my big brother was so cool, he was a proper athlete. We were ducking, diving, running likkle joke till he got me. After that, all I could do was cry like a bitch all the way home. At seven, seeing all that blood, I'm surprised I didn't pass out. When we got home, my brother, stuttering and shook to death, explained how it happened, then Dad told him, 'You stupid boy, look what you done to his arm. Go get the tow rope for your beating.' I felt bad cause I was playing too, but that's how it went. My brother was older, he should have known better and that's why he got wet tow rope all over his arse. My Dad was a mechanic so tow rope was always around and by the way my brother screamed, I could tell it gave a good lash. I think my Dad liked beating him. My brother just playing arcade games would be enough sometimes. As I think back on it, it's tru, my Dad was pissed with his own life my brother got it the way he did. It never had anything to do with my brother staying out late, it was probably more about my brother wasting money. The money my Dad would have wasted instead after extorting Mum.

I remember Dad bare times, walking up and down talking under his breath till he had enough of waiting, then he'd go out and get him. He knew my brother would be playing the arcade at the top of the hill in the chip shop, so he'd sneak up on him and startle him with a lash. My brother would have to run leave the game, getting lashed all the way home.

BASICS ON THE ENDZ

CHAPTER TWO

We lived in a two bedroom house in Walthamstow, East London. It weren't nothing special, but we had the basics and this black cat I used to terrorize by sitting on it all the time. I loved that cat, I don't know why I used to do that. It ran away after a while, probably because I almost suffocated it bare times. At the time, I thought the cat liked it.

I don't know how life was for my brother before I came - other than obviously he had his own bedroom - but from what I could see my brother had it hard. I never got the beatings he got. All I remembered was good times with my Dad, in the beginning anyway while he was there. Even when he taught me how to ride a bike it was jokes. There weren't no stabilisers on a brand new kiddies' bike. It was one rusty old woman's bike with a puffy seat, he taught me on. He took me to the top of a concrete hill and pushed me down it till I learnt. After a few knee scrape boo-boos, jumping off clean and landing on my feet became a necessity, before I mastered my balance. At home, I noticed quickly I was my Dad's favourite. In the evening, most nights me and him would squeeze up in the likkle one-piece sofa and leave Mumsy and my brother on the three-piece. My brother must have resented me for that. It must have been all about him before I came a long, tru our older sister on Mum's side came up in Barbados with the rest of Mum's family.

Around the age seven and a half I started noticing my parents had a problem. I didn't know why they were arguing so much at first, but as weeks past, I realised Mumsy left each morning bright and early to go work and she worked hard to support us in all kind of weather. Dad on the other hand, I'm not gonna say he didn't work, but, I'd say he definitely didn't work as hard as Mum. It all came out on my eighth birthday, *just how hard he'd been working*, when I was due to have my birthday party. We had to cancel because he hadn't paid the electric bill. Mumsy had to lie to the parents. My Dad was making joke until my uncle showed up. He couldn't let him in tru the shame. I didn't get it fully at the time but I remember being upset, all my friends coming round and we weren't even allowed to play.

Them times der, the man dem were Jonathon, Daniel and Simeon. My god brothers, we called each other 'cousins'. Any time I could chill with them man I would. They didn't live far from me, but I weren't allowed to go there on my own so it was a Christmas, Easter and summer holiday ting and I never wanted to leave. We'd be ramping from morning to night, playing hide and seek in all the clothes around the house. Pillow fights on the bed, in between Amstrad and Commodore 64 - them old game consoles that took cassette tape where we had to cross our fingers and wait about ten minutes for it to load. Games like Yie Ar Kung-Fu and Athletics where your fingers would mash up by the time you finished playing them, *bare pressing button*, or we'd ride our bikes down Copper Mill Lane, through the marshes up into Tottenham or Hackney depending what direction we decided to go; underneath railway tracks with whole heap of rats, up and down crazy hills, it was jokes. We didn't give a shit about the time, not even food. We'd only know it was time to go home when the sun went down. Their house felt together in a funny kind of way, as hard as life was for them. Something was always going on, even though it weren't always good. *Family spirit they had round there, with their sugar-water.*

That was holiday time. But during the week and Saturday's I'd be kicking ball with my friends Jimmy, Justin and the twins in Red Head Primary School. Sunday was chill day with Nicky B and his family after church.

WHY DAD?

CHAPTER THREE

It was a few months after my birthday, with my parents' relationship getting worse, when one night we woke up to Mumsy screaming,

'WHY YOU DOING THIS TO ME, PLEASE NO, DON'T!'

My Dad had poured petrol all over her screaming,

'YOU THINK YOU CAN EMBARRASS ME INFRONT OF MY FRIENDS, BITCH, I'LL FUCKING KILL YOU IN HERE, FUCKING WITH ME!'

He was trying to tie her to the bed. Mumsy jumped up, in fear for her life fighting. Dad had lost control and my brother was thinking about jumping out the window. I think he just wanted an excuse to see if he could. I weren't jumping.

My Dad had been trying to extort Mumsy to start a business with some drunk brea (random person). It weren't even like Mumsy was saying *No*, she just wanted to see a contract or something. My Dad didn't know nothing about contracts though and he didn't have his own money so he was telling her basically, 'If you don't give me that money, watch what happens to you.' This is why they were fighting that night and trust me, they fought hard. After all that, even I knew Mumsy couldn't stay with him so a few days later she filed for divorce. Around the same time, Jimmy moved off the endz (local area) to South End. And then I heard Johnathon, Simeon, Daniel and the rest of the family were moving too.

Within a week or so, the letter from the solicitor came telling Dad it was official. I came in from school to see him sitting on the bed, crying. He asked me if I knew what was going on. I said 'No', but I did. I remember thinking, *what the fuck did you expect, beating Mumsy like that?* Then he asked me who I wanted to stay with. I didn't say anything, but we both knew I'd be rolling with Mum. He was cool and shit, but I knew he weren't serious. Then he asked me and my brother to talk Mumsy into letting him stay. He even went to the church for help. When that didn't work, Mumsy thought he tried to poison her. She don't know what he put in the food, but as she cooked some meat, she thought it weren't cooking right so she left it in the pot. When my brother got in from school, he ate some and it fucked him up. It's lucky he didn't eat much. Dad said 'I didn't do anything to the meat' so no one knew.

In that same week Dad overdosed on pills. He must have been desperate, I don't know what he was thinking, but by that time, Mumsy didn't give a shit and probably wished he would just hurry up and die. Nothing worked for him and within a month everything was done. A few weeks after that, we were looking for a new house and Dad was getting restraining orders, telling him shit like 'You're not allowed within fifty meters of any of them.' We looked at a few spots on the endz and found one we liked, so we moved in about a month later. It was a nicer, bigger house, but things changed quickly when we moved there. Johnathon, Daniel, Simeon and Jimmy were gone, I was in a different area. Still in Walthamstow but not that close for a little man like me, so I needed my brother more than ever all now, but he weren't thinking about me. He bounced to do his own ting. Tru he was coming on seventeen, eight years older than me, what he was on didn't include his little brother.

MY GIRL

CHAPTER FOUR

This is when I met Donnie. Donnie's brother and my brother came up together as yutes. He had a little crew on the endz and I needed someone to show me wha gwan so he ended up playing big brother for a while. Donnie was five years older than me and rolling with him I even found me a little girlfriend. G. She was a proper, pretty little thing. Brown skin, a few inches shorter than me, I didn't know what I was doing with her, but G was my girl and I was feeling her.

It was around the time, Thatcher was controlling shit with that iron fist. The endz were Conservative, upper class, lower class and under class. Most of the parents I knew were members of that under class and wanted acceptance within society so bad, they would do almost anything for it; but no Blacks, Irish or dogs was the reality of racism where I lived.

In the first summer holiday after I moved, but before I started secondary school, the local park was the spot for us yutes. Growing up in London, there weren't much for an inner-city yute to do. That's why going park and getting chased by half-dead dogs seemed like fun and them half-dead dogs chased us regular.

I learnt some valuable lessons though, as a yute man in them early days rolling with Donnie and his crew. One evening, this dog was on road roaming like it did when it ended up on the block where Donnie lived. Me and Donnie were there chilling, then the dog just started trying to attack him. It was clearly trying to bite Donnie, it had nothing to do with me. I'm just there thinking, FUCK!!!!.....   This guy grabs me and pushed me in the way for the dog to bite me instead. He was a lot stronger than me, so there was nothing I could do other than think *what a bastard* as I shouted 'Get Off Me!' The dog didn't get me but it was trying.

I had my first little girlfriend too and even though I was shy, I thought she was gonna be my girl forever. One of the 'olders' had an eye on her though and when it was time for me to go home, this guy was around, trying it, so it didn't take long before I had no girl. I hated her for a long time for dumping me, but what could I do. He was an older man for me, his game was tighter than mine and he was telling her shit she wanted to hear. I learnt right there, you can't take a girl that don't want to be taken.

After getting dumped, when I got home, laying in bed at nine years old I remembered the old days. I wondered wha gwan for John and them, they were like brothers to me. I thought about that party Mumsy's work friend's daughter had, over in South a few years before. It was live, she had all her friends round and Jonathon was breaking them Michael Jackson moves, giving man jokes. I smiled as I remembered these yutes climbing the wall in the passage. I remembered thinking, *is that allowed*. I'd never even thought about doing that shit in my house, but the way these yutes were climbing the wall comfortable and shit I thought it must be cool, so I started doing it too. I was having the worl (a lot) of fun until her dad caught me. Just me he caught doing shit too! I couldn't say I thought it was alright, *it weren't in my house*. My fun got cancelled for the rest of that night. I had to sit and watch. I felt like crying that night as I reminisced cause I missed them man still.

WHY?

CHAPTER FIVE

When I moved, I had to change school and everything. South Grove was my school. I was there most of my life. Obviously I didn't want to leave the school and yutes I had come up with. I missed 'next door', that's what I called her. She lived next door to me at our old house and looked after me when my Dad was out doing shit. I only had two years left before secondary school, so I ended up in Roger Asham, the school two minutes from my new yard (house).

That's when I met Squeaks. We called him Squeaks cause even though we were all young, his pitch was noticeably high. He didn't go Roger Asham anymore, but he lived across the road so we would link up after school and chill certain times. In school, me and Robert were the main guys in my year. There was one half decent teacher too, but other than them, nothing was going on for Roger Asham. During school, Mumsy would be at work, working hard. She worked two jobs to provide for us. Her main job was working for the government in their transport department. Her second job was cleaning the office she worked in before she started work.

When school finished, I stayed out till hunger sent my

arse home getting into trouble with Robert as long as possible - Mumsy moaning was already starting to get on my nerves. I felt like she hated me. She couldn't see I was a good yute, always shouting at me for random shit. I didn't know what I had done, but as time went on, I thought I must remind her of my Dad. *I might of hated me too, if I was her*. Reading was the other thing-'You must read, Christopher!' she used to tell me all the time. She sounded like a broken record with all that read talk. Her life weren't great; we didn't have everything we needed, so I had to wonder how comes books hadn't taken us out the struggle. I thought, if books lead to cleaning the office you work in to earn extra cash, so you complain you don't have enough, you can keep them fucking books!

I could never say she didn't try with us though, she cooked, cleaned and got my shit ready for school like a Mum supposed to, but it always seemed like I was the worst guy. It might have been, she hated that after everything she done for me... I still had so much love for him. Or maybe it was something else. Whatever it was, she made it clear she thought I was going to be just like my worthless nigga father, *as she called him sometimes*. The problem with that is, when you hear it enough you start believing it. So I was soon well on my way to becoming just what Mumsy told me I would. It only took a few months before I saw how drastic things had changed. My Dad was really gone, with the restraining orders. My brother met some chick and before he knew her a week he was living with her in her yard. I understood why my brother left. I just wished he had spared a thought for little me.

I had other family in London too but they weren't around me either, it was just me. When I asked about my Dad, Mumsy said, 'You won't be seeing him again until you old enough to see him on your own.' I stopped asking about him after that cause reality set in and I realised, it was me one rolling all now. And that's where road life started for me. It came from feeling like Mumsy didn't want me around. I was soon learning the cold hard realities of London life, where people were starving, envious and bad mind and boy dem (police) encouraged Blacks to victimise other Blacks.

HELP

CHAPTER SIX

By now I had made some friends on my road and at the weekend I'd be playing football with them if Squeaks or Robert weren't around. I was getting older and a little more confident so Mumsy said on this one weekend, I could go to Walthamstow Market and play the arcade games. One Irish yute I played football with was allowed to come too, so that was us. We went down to the market with about ten pounds each and we were playing this new game that had just come out called Street Fighter. This game was wicked, totally revolutionary to the games we were used to from back in the day. I was feeling real all now with this yute. We wanted some sweets, so we left the arcade to go get some and that's when some bigger yutes ambushed us. They must have been watching us for a minute, so when we got to a little quiet spot where not much people were around, they muscled us behind a wall so no one could see wha gwan and they had us there talking. One of them said, 'Oi, how much money you got.' I could see what was happening so I saw an opportunity to run and get some help. But I got blocked in by a van and one of them caught me. He brought me back and threw me on the floor, saying 'Don't do that again!' They peeled our pockets back and took all our money. I had about nine pound left on me and I was pissed! I think they went back to the arcades to play that Street Fighter with our money. I just wanted to go home after that.

Times like that, I wished my brother was about - we could have gone back and fucked them up. But he weren't. When I got home I told Mumsy. I could see she was shocked. She didn't know what to say. She just said,'So!' That one hurt. A little later, I knocked for that yute I was with and his mum came to the door with a knife talking about 'Don't you ever take my son anywhere ever again, do you hear me?' I said, 'Ok.' After that I weren't knocking for him again!

SUFFERING IN SILENCE

CHAPTER SEVEN

Things weren't good all now and I was suffering in silence. After Donnie would have let that dog bite me, we slowly stopped linking and him and his bredrins were on different tings now they were getting older too. All we still did together was play some football on Regents Place, but that weren't often anymore.

Regents Place was where I met the Gamble family. David was my age, he'd come play ball with us. Maria was a year older, Mark was a lot older and a proper big brother to David and Maria. Mark knew my brother from Boys' Brigade. Howard was the oldest brother I knew, but they had older brothers I didn't know. Mark was the man on Regents Place, he always had man dem in and out his yard. He sold stuff, green mainly, but other things too and everyone on the endz passed through at some point. I used to love chilling with dem man. It was active, their mum and dad were both cool, but the dad was a drunk. He gave their mum trouble sometimes but it didn't matter to me - their dysfunctional house was better than mine. I knew when I met Mark, him and some of his man dem were gonna show me wha gwan.

That New Year's Eve 1989, I'm eleven all now and Mark decided I was old enough to roll with him and the olders for the night. David weren't on it, but I was. I couldn't believe my own brother had never invited me to roll with him like this, but Marky was letting me come. I loved Marky for that, I ain't gonna lie. First we went West End and ended up at Spotlight. The security was talking some £35 to get in talk. I didn't have that - I weren't sure who did - but that weren't the one. We jumped back in the whip (car) and two two's we were in New Cross, round the front of Ghetto Estate. That was the first real dance I went to. I remember getting there thinking, *fuck me! I need stay close to the man dem.* All I could see was bare tugs (thugs). It was New Cross, Peckham and Lewisham yutes controlling that dance. I didn't know much about them yutes at the time, but I could see the endz where grimy. Weed smoke filled the air, I was used to the earthy natural aroma from all the days at Marks yard and I loved it. It was a Westwood dance and he drew a crowd. I used to hear him on the radio, now I was in his dance *feeling real.* This raving ting was me, skanking (dancing) in the dance with man dem giggling, new chicks all around. I started walking around, chilling in corners on my own running joke with sexy chicks, feeling their bums while I'm dancing with them. I was moving! Mark could see I was a raver by how he had to look around to see me scrubbing chicks down, giving man winks like, *I'm bless cuz.* I was on it! I weren't smoking weed yet, but I loved the smell. It chilled me out, I was at home inside the dance for real. It's just a shame some guys couldn't just enjoy themselves without popping shit off.

We were in there a few hours then the first beef kicked off and the dance got gassed. One guy got it but the gas affected everyone so we had to come out. My eye's were burning and I couldn't breathe properly for a bit but other than that, I was cool and I linked the man dem up outside.

They were all cool too so we had a giggle about what happened, then in the New Year's spirit when the gas cleared the dance got cracking again. So we went back in and got back to it, skanking feeling brand new, until more beef kicked off. This time it was bottles. One guy got bottled and that's when the dance done. As the guy was being taken out, glass still in his face and blood all over him, I remember wondering *why*. I didn't know back then what life had in store for us and being Black was a crime, but I was soon learning the hard way. *It's a shame some of us never learned.*

PECKING ORDER

1990

CHAPTER EIGHT

Roger Asham in that New Year flew by and before I knew it secondary school was round the corner. Getting ready to leave Roger Asham, it was all about Holy Family College. McKenty was the school on my bits, round the corner from my yard that I wanted to go to, but Mumsy weren't having it. She had heard it had a bad reputation and too many bad boys went there. She thought Holy Family was the good Catholic school I needed. It weren't even negotiable. I wondered why Mumsy always fucked with my shit. Most of my people were going McKenty, or already went there, so I was pissed. I knew by the time I got home, dem man would have left already. But at the same time, Squeaks was going Holy Family and I knew it was time for me to flap my wings, so I ended up just accepting it. I knew me and the main McKenty man would still link up on the weekend and holidays anyway.

But still, in the beginning of my Holy Family days, sometimes I would rush back to catch McKenty man leaving, tru I finished ten minutes before them and the site I was at was quite near to my house. David was still foundation man dem, but I saw we were on different tings when we started secondary school, cause he was cool chilling on the block and I saw this as the time to start seeing what's good on the endz.

McKenty had some big Walthamstow man going there all now and the guys I already knew, knew them. So it wasn't long before I met man like Oki and Dragon. Oki was the barber and Dragon was his right-hand man. I originally started linking Oki for trims because my old barber Edds, one of Mark's people got more busy and harder to get hold of. Mark could trim too, but he weren't around really anymore either cause he was with his new chick.

And Scalp him killer B, the parents' favourite. I had had enough of his fuck-ups, especially if I didn't go with my Mum, the trim would take ten minutes and it was always dead. He couldn't fade like us yutes wanted and he couldn't do designs. I asked this guy to give me a high-top fade with BMW sign in the back of my head one time. KMFT! I felt like crying when he finished that one and he had the nerve to charge me extra.

When Oki gave me that first bad boy trim with designs and decent fade he was the man. Saturday was the day we would trim, if we didn't catch him on Friday after school. Then we hit road trying to steal whatever we could along the way always heading to Trocadero, tru it was the spot for us youngers. The crew became the man that Oki trimmed on the weekend and as time went on and Oki trimmed more man, the crew got bigger. In the beginning it was Me, Oki, Jubs, Justin from Red Head days, Dragon, Abbs, Play, Clayton, Bigger, Quarms and Nats. Del lived round the corner from Oki, but went to a school off the endz so he rolled with a different crew. Moreno, Pepper, Risky and them Islington man were his man dem, but they were cool so after a while we all started rolling. A few of the man dem like Bigger, Jubs and Abbs were a little older, so they were a little more advanced. I did watch them man still, they made me know I needed to up my game.

Us man from early had bare girls, that's what we were known for. When we used to end up at Trocadero on a Saturday, we would always take bare numbers, sometimes we would take the girls home the same night. I remember one night, Abbs brought this random chick back to the endz after drawing her in Trocadero. He beat (had sex) her in the base with all us man next door. Even though I was still a virgin, I liked that move. And I knew it wouldn't be long before I was the joke, if I just kept watching man fuck and didn't start fucking.

A few weeks later I was there at Trocadero and I saw this chick watching me. She was decent, a slim light-skin ting, quite tall with shoulder length hair and a little back-off (arse). There wasn't a reason why I couldn't talk to her, so I went and had a word. Her name was Shola. By the time I finished with her, I swear I had swag. It's the way she quickly gave me her number and told me, 'Make sure you phone me you know!' I gave her a cool, 'I definitely will babes' and walked off back to the man dem, who were all watching. They shouted 'Gwan Sibs', that was my road name all now. I giggled but I was shy and they were making too much noise, but I played cool and kept it moving like it was nothing.

DIDN'T KNOW

CHAPTER NINE

In school on the Monday, I came in with a new swag. I remember man even asking me what happened over the weekend cause I looked happy. I said, 'yeah man, I had a nice weekend still'. Holy Family College, it was live; it weren't the kind of school you would have expected it to be with a name like that. It seemed like a lot of Black parents from the endz thought that a 'good Catholic' school was what we needed. That must have been what attracted all the bad yutes' to that 'good Catholic' school. At break and dinner time, I couldn't see anything religious going on round there, shit was cracking. Fighting, stealing and robbing instigated mostly by our olders, was all that was going on. And we didn't know about the paedophilic behaviour going on in the Catholic church yet.

We had two sites: Us youngers stayed on the new site for the first two years with the six-form pussy holes. I was class of 1990. In the beginning, we had a few live man in my year. Me, Squeaks, Langer, El and Tin. Then there was Big T, Charlie and Lindon, I had love for Lindon. His dad was a martial arts expert, so a serious disciplinarian. We had man like Josh, he reminded me of Gile in Street Fighter. The first guy that made me see how small the world is. Then there was O'Neil, this guy, he ended up being one of my best friends after I gave him a little beating for troubling Squeaks. I went and elbow-dropped him, obviously he didn't like that, so he came at me like he wanted to do something. I gave him kick-jab-cross then skipped on him like Ali. I was quick, way too quick for O'Neil, but after that, we became friends. We all made sure Gareth a next yute was nice - he had Sickle Cell. Merv, he used to wear shoes at least two sizes bigger than his foot. He looked like a clown in the early days, one of them guys in the *Kia-Ora* advert we used to love, always with his basketball. Those were the main guys in my year; there were others but they either weren't in my class, or they didn't make enough noise to be noticed in them early days.

The top girls in my year were Shelly, Reanna, Ester and Joy. Shelly loved me off – she was sexy and all that too. It's just that she rocked her hair natural, which weren't a bad thing but I didn't know that yet. She had this band she used to wear round the front, I weren't feeling too. Reanna now, she had her hair relaxed from morning; we were all feeling her in my year and every man was on her. Shelly was playing number two to Reanna in the early days, tru that and Reanna was shy so she was safe. I think she liked me too, but nothing was going on cause we weren't in the same class, so I couldn't really try it.

Ester was like one of the man dem, she was big-boned and no one was on her. She used to get touchy real quick too, she might have whacked you up so no one really pushed her buttons too much. Jennifer came in as the new girl when we were settled and everyone knew their place. She was a straight-off-the-boat Nigerian and we took the piss out of her accent from she landed for the longest while. We called her De Titty cause her tits were big back then. But as we got to know her she was cool. There were a few other girls there, but they were the main chicks in my year.

We were the teachers' nightmare, that's why they split us up. We done a lot of shit to them all the time and threw chairs at them regular. One of our favourites was putting shit in their hot drinks, it seemed like they enjoyed that shit more when we did. We always got Mr Times with that one. He was a tall fagot-looking brea that loved to fuck with us. He was a lot bigger than most of us and he could shout, so he wouldn't have it in his class. Every class without fail, we'd wait for him to leave. He thought he had control like that and he could just leave the class and come back and we'd all just be getting on with his work. That pussy was wrong, we hated him and how he'd try to have us up. So, that's why we'd spit in his drink or put shit in it – stir it around with whatever science equipment we had on the dirty school tables and watch him enjoy. We couldn't make him cry or run for back-up like a lot of the others, so that was how he got it.

We were always laughing about something. We destroyed the lessons where we didn't respect the teachers. Man like Mr Hecks our P.E. teacher, he was cool. Or Mr Darnis and Mr Queenie, they were hard-back Black teachers that were having nothing. These teachers showed you respect, as long as you respected them. Playing cards in their lessons would easily get you the chalkboard cleaner in your head. I got that a few times before I learnt. I felt like fighting them sometimes when the whole class would buss up laughing at me, but I respected them so I would leave it. *I knew I was doing wrong!* Mrs Chapping taught IT and we all liked IT, so we didn't give her much trouble. Mr Harry now, he was some half-blind brea; we didn't like him but we had to re-spect him. It's like he had a military background, so if you done something and he was around, he was coming for you and you were doing detention.

It was about fifty percent white and fifty percent mixed

with all other ethnic groups in Holy Family. I would say Blacks made up about twenty percent of that; but us Black yutes were weighty in my school. What potential we had. I didn't know it then in my conscious, but my subconscious knew something weren't right, with what them teachers were teaching us. They were teaching us bullshit, none of that real shit you need to join that one percent that had almost half the world's wealth. Nothing about assets, it was all about liability and debt. Good slaves they were teaching us to be when I check it, not just the Black yutes, all of us. That's the reason us popular yutes fucked around in class. You could tell half of them didn't want to be there teaching us anyway.

TELL THE TRUTH

CHAPTER TEN

For me as a Black yute, I would have engaged more and tried harder if they had given me a less bias Black history to work with. It ain't like we didn't have no inspirational shit to talk about. That would have inspired me, but they didn't want that. They liked Black's learning slavery, torture and rape and how they divide to conquer us. When they taught us about Africa, it come like Africa was a bad word and Roots was all we needed. They could have taught us about the Moors and how we controlled the world for years, civilizing the uncivilized. It was well known then like it is now that Africa is the beginning of civilisation, so why not tell us that. Man like Mansa Musa, the richest man that ever lived. Queen Nzinga the real Warrior Princess. The countless African Empires from The Ethiopian and Benin to The Zulu and The Asante, The Mali and Songhai, The Mossi Kingdoms, to name a few. All the teachings we brought the world in Religion, Astrology, Architecture, Fine Arts and Craft. Or if that was too much for them, they could have taught us about man like *John Hanson* the (real) first ever President of The United States of America. The countless Black inventors that had helped make the world what it is today. It's obvious someone didn't want productive pro-gressive yutes. The school-to-prisons pipeline agenda made more sense. I used to wonder why some of those teachers hated us so bad but it weren't even personal, them teachers weren't that smart. All they were guilty of was racism. They didn't know the syllabus was full of shit - it didn't even teach western ideals of success. The teachers were the front line in the war of suppression. Any chance they got they tried to break our spirit. From early it was teachers against students! So we enjoyed finding ways of saying fuck you.

It turned out to be a vicious circle though, because after you've just pissed a teacher off real bad or even worse, made one of them cry, that would be the excuse for them to fuck you over even more. The fact that they were adults and should have known better didn't mean shit, they tried to fuck you and they tried to do that to all of us - with no thought or care for our future.

I remember my football team went to play one school off the endz one day. The RE teacher Mr James turned football coach, for some stupid reason. I don't know what the fuck this guy knew about football - he hadn't even seen us play - but he subbed me straight away. Half-time, we 3 – null down and I'm thinking, *put me on*. I could have turned it around but instead he put on some funny brea that didn't even play football. The pussy didn't even play me. He al-ways thought I was flash, so I think he done that to show me I was replaceable. I resented him for that and I never played football for the school again.That guy possibly changed my career.

DAWG

CHAPTER ELEVEN

The year was 1991 and I hadn't seen my brother for over a year, I had learnt to live without him. I had his bedroom all now too and even though he had indirectly helped me, I couldn't see it at the time, because I was earning my own stripes (respect). Mumsy told me one evening, 'Andrew's coming home, him and his girlfriend have broken up.' I thought, *as long as he ain't trying to take back his bedroom, I don't care*. The time of needing and missing him had gone. I was on my own ting now.

I remember the day Mumsy told me because it was the same day Little had beef with Charlie. Little was a bad yute from the endz, on this road ting from early. He carried his borer (knife) everywhere, so when I heard Little's gonna fight Charlie, I wanted to see. Little didn't go to our school; he weren't old enough to go secondary school yet, but he'd been expelled from so many schools already, he weren't even going school. I don't know why Charlie and Little had beef, but Charlie had a big mouth, so I could only assume that had something to do with it. They linked up in the playground at lunch time and Little gave D (one of the olders) his borer, then moved to Charlie quickly. Charlie should have done better than that. He basically just stood there and took a beating.

The next day after school when I came home, my brother was there. I weren't sure how to feel seeing him again after all this time. I thought *he didn't care about me, why should I care about him*. But I did care! He was in the front room chilling, I said,'Wha gwan bruv, you cool?'

He said,'Yeah, what happening?'

I said,'Nothing much, just school innit'; then I went upstairs to check he hadn't moved my shit. He hadn't and I remember thinking, *I know he's pissed*, that room he is in all now was tiny. I wondered, *is he gonna be my big brother now, or the same guy that left me when he went to do his own ting*. It didn't take long for me to work that out. From the day he got back, he was out. I hardly saw him. He really didn't give a shit about me and I could see that clearly now. It hurt me but I couldn't let him see that, I couldn't let no one see that. Fuck it I thought, I don't need him for anything, but deep down it hurt me a lot.

He'd been back about a week all now and I remember it was a cold Friday evening. I heard the gate open and it didn't just sound like my brother at the door. I thought he must have brought one of his friends home, but when he opened the door and I see this big old German Shepherd gallop into the yard I'm thinking, *what the fuck is this*? I said, 'Whose dog's that bruv?'

He said, 'Mine.'

I said,'Does Mum know?'

'Yeah' he said.

Dawg looked like he had a permanent smile and bare energy. JR, one of my brother's bredrin - his mum had had enough of Dawg, its bad habits and size. I could see her point still, Dawg was crazy. For the first few weeks, Dawg was eating my food off my plate any chance it got. Imagine, I'm hungry, ain't eaten all day. After a while and a lot of licks (beatings), he didn't stop doing it, he just accepted the fact that sometimes he was just gonna get a beating. I just had to remember to put my food somewhere he couldn't get it or take it with me. He'd go hide if he'd done something wrong when we got home, that's how we'd know he needed a beating. Dawg would tremble and walk when we called him. *That shit was funny.*

I ain't gonna lie, I quickly grew to love Dawg.

A LITTLE NERVOUS

CHAPTER TWELVE

This was around the time I had my little girl friend Shola, she was really feeling me all now. She used to make sure she was always at Trocadero on a Saturday cause she knew that's where I'd be. Me and my crew, we were hot boys. All the Trocadero girls loved us off. She was making them know though, I was her man. I did like her, she was definitely alright but tru she was older than me, she wanted me in ways I weren't ready for yet. It's tru I was still a virgin, the thought of what I knew she wanted made me nervous. I was scared and my little issue with G had me questioning myself. Now too much time had passed and I was starting to feel like I was looking like a fag. So I told her I had another girl. I remember her crying 'big cry' as she got on the bus leaving my house. She was a good girl and the fact she still gave me a little chain she got for me, made me know that. I knew I was gonna miss her, but the truth was, I was learning that the only thing certain in life was change.

That Monday after I broke up with Shola, I was chilling with the Second years and realised the time was coming for them man to leave and go to the old site as Third years. I thought to myself, *it's gonna be fucking dead in here when you man leave*. Them Second years kept the school live with the serious man they had in that year. They actually controlled our site with the Sixth formers included. They taught us how to scam the buses and Trivial Pursuit McDonald's scratch cards. We were learning more life skills from them than the teachers, so I wondered what the fuck we was gonna do. My year was looking like a joke all now, cause they had already managed to kick Langer, El and Tin out for theft, accusations of rape and intimidation; so the top boys left were only me and Squeaks really.

As for my brother, after a while I weren't feeling him being back. He was trying to play dad. If I got in trouble, he gave me the wire. If Mumsy grounded me, I weren't going nowhere and summer was here. This summer I could see shit was really gonna get cracking as well. The crew was big all now and it was just us youngers on road doing our ting. I could see my brother fucking with that shit if he stayed around. I wanted to rave my life away in those Hackney dances wid man like Mad Cobra, Super Cat, Shabba, Ninja Man, Buju, Tupac, Biggie, Mob Deep, Black Moon, Dr Dre, LL Cool J, smashing up big dances like Rosemary. Us man had no business in Rosemary's in them early days, we were too young, but we were there skanking feeling real with big DJ's like Rampage. Then Ashwin Street came along for us man, with man like Fresh Finger Al mixing it down nice and Junior Dangerous on the mic. Ashwin Street was more our time. All the younger Hackney, Tottenham, Waltham-stow, Leyton and Leytonstone man were der for Ashwin Street. You might have got wet or bored up in them dances, but London was serious; it's just how it went on the endz certain times.

Memories of the first time we touched Ashwin Street always brings a smile to my face. We got inside, it was what you call a shoobs. Very dingy, there was nothing nice about Ashwin Street, but we didn't care. It was just bad boy youngers up inside. We got a drink and found a spot near the DJ booth. I didn't know Al yet, but I wanted to see who mixed it down cause he had the crowd locked in. I'm looking over and it's a little dark, but in the corner sitting down it looked like Squeaks I could see. I thought it was him because of the hairstyle he had at the time, a little slant that was plaited. I'm there looking for a minute, I said, 'That's Squeaks tarass, *that's actually Squeaks!*' I approached him slowly cause I still couldn't believe it and said, 'Yo, wha gwan!'

He looked at me in shock, I could see his face said, *'what you doing here?'* I was thinking the same thing I'm not gonna lie. He was der with Big Al! He asked me, 'Who you with?' I showed him the man dem. Since we had started in Holy Family, Squeaks had moved back to his mum's house round the corner from school, so he didn't know I had crew like that. We hadn't rolled outside of school since Roger Asham. But from that night, Squeaks was back rolling with man full-time.

I remember we touched Brockwell Park all-dayer, the first time that year too. It was in Brixton, the heart of the Twenty-Eights endz. Them man had a serious crew so they run their block, they actually had London shook in the Nineties, them and The Untouchables another Brixton crew. Back then, if you heard them man were coming for you, you needed help and big-guns cause some of them man were killers.

WHY'S HE BEGGING?

CHAPTER THIRTEEN

We left our block late waiting on Oki to finish trimming everyone. We still had a few hours and the weather was nice, so we knew it was still good to go. From we passed Oxford Street we could feel the energy like you would have expected it to be at Carnival. We got to Brixton and what could I say, it was very live over there. You could hear Ninja Man banging from the station. Westwood was mixing it down and there were bare girls around - our kind of vibe - so we were always staying till the end. I was actually pissed when it finished cause us man were warming up nice, but we were going out that evening so the party weren't done. We started heading back to the endz cause we needed to get changed and chill for a bit. By the time we were leaving, we were rolling about forty man strong. The train was packed with us man and tru the sun was out everyting was nice – we were having a good time as well, until some prick lost his mind. This guy thought it was cool to come up behind Squeaks and high-kicked him off the train for holding the door. He kicked Squeaks in his back with so much force, if I weren't standing there, Squeaks would have flown into the chocolate machine. Then he started laughing like it was some kind of joke. We hadn't even said nothing to the prick even though he had kept the door open the stop before and now he's trying to take man for dickhead like this. Squeaks turned and looked at him as the door closed, we were pissed, all we could do was call him a pussy hole. He was never getting away with it, we had bare man on that train. But we wanted to beat him as well, it's a good thing one of the man dem, Sifa, was on the next carriage talking to someone else. He was keeping his door open too. When Sif see what happened he said, 'Yo Sibs, Squeaks, come this way!' When that prick saw us getting back on the train, his ass fell out. We jumped back on the train quick and opened the door to that carriage where this pussy hole was. Squeaks was in a hurry! By this point the prick was begging, 'I'M SORRY, PLEASE PLEASE DON'T' HURT ME!'

Squeaks punched his begging mouth closed as he talked his shit, then everyone swallowed him up. There was so many man on him, some man didn't get him properly. Good practice was three man, that's all you needed to give a man a real beating cause everyone had space to work on a different body part. But it was the violation that made everyone want to beat this guy. No-bystander tried to help him either cause they all saw what happened. They see him take the piss and they see him get exactly what he needed. We left him fucked up on the floor. All Squeaks had been doing was telling me he wanted to link me for the evening, tru we were going Cheese's dance in Shepherd's Bush. Me and a few man had decided to get off at Highbury & Islington on a quick one to go try make some money. After that, we went about our business and linked up in the evening at Oxford Street, slyly looking trouble. We got on the Central line going West – pissed with what had happened, we hadn't started no trouble and mans taking us for dick heads.

Towards the end of the journey, the train comes out of the

tunnel. This brea was sitting there minding his business and we just started fucking with him. He weren't having it, so we gave him a beating. As we were beating him, someone pulled the emergency lever, but we didn't know till the train pulled into White City station and the doors weren't opening. We thought, *shit, we better split up* but we were all still on the train. Boy dem were going to talk to the man, round us up and take us to jail for GBH.

With Abbs I said, 'Fuck it,' and slipped through the separation between carriages on to the platform. I'd never done that before, but Abbs, he done that like he done that ting regular. Tru I was skinny it was easy for me to slip through too. As we walked towards the stairs to leave the platform, I looked on to the train and see man dem panicking. I made eye contact wid Squeaks and giggled as I mouthed, 'Phone when you get out.' Thinking they might go jail. They looked pissed to see me and Abbs strolling out all cool and shit. As we headed for the exit, we see boy dem and dogs coming. I thought *shit*, but they just let us walk past. I forgot the doors were still closed; how could it have been us they were looking for. It's a good thing Abbs knew them endz, cause I didn't know where the fuck we were going, we walked for miles. The guy saw us as we strolled off, so he must have told the boy dem they missed us cause no one got shift. We all linked back up at Hammersmith train station where the dance was and went in feeling real.

ALL-DAYERS

CHAPTER FOURTEEN

So now we in the dance skanking big skank going on with tings, giggling, drawing new West London chicks. Cheese's dance was popping and everything was nice until someone gassed the place and done the dance. We were pissed, now we in West London and the dance is done. Cheese's dances usually finished at 6:00am, so we could jump on the first train back to the endz, but now we having to jump on night bus. We never thought about that shit, we were crazy back then, jumping on trains to any part of London to rave with no clue how we were gonna get back to the endz, but it was fun. Even in the rain, we lived with that shit cause we didn't know any better. It took us about two and a half hours to get back that night.

Summer, early Nineties all-dayers were the ting us man done. It's like we went to a different one every weekend. The only problem was, everyone we went to, shit popped off. Yutes were coming up and everyone wanted to make a name for their self. Everyone had a big ego so we started carrying borers, one pops guns and gas. It made us feel a likkle more comfy still. And after a while, my brother cooled down his 'You going to listen to me and do what I say' bullshit. He weren't home often enough to be telling me what and what I can do, so I had time to breathe again.

Summer holiday was over now and we were getting ready to go back to school. It was always a depressing time. The weather was about to turn shit again, and we'd have to go back to this bullshit routine none of us liked.

2ND YEAR OF
HOLY FAMILY

CHAPTER FIFTEEN

Back to school in the Second year, I knew it was gonna be boring, but fuck me, it really was when our olders left. Our site had Sixth formers, you would have thought that would have meant something, but that didn't mean shit - them guys were pussy if you ask me. I thought that from First year. Why would you go to our Sixth-form when Waltham Forest College or even Monoux was round the corner? And that's just two, for a young man trying to find himself; and that's only if you decided to stay on the endz. Most of them were weak and scared, that's why they stayed. I didn't like them either, after one of them punched me up cause I called him a pussy. He used to walk like a boss, but he looked like a faggot. One day I said to him, 'Why are you here? Shouldn't you be in a proper college? I think you're a pussy, you're scared and you can't manage a proper college. Us youngers run this site.' After he punched me up, I went and told the others and just like the pussy I thought he was, I never saw him again for the rest of the year.

It was just about us and our youngers after that. Back then I saw them all as pipsqueaks. In their year though, there was quite a few of them. They had a few decent chicks too, but I weren't watching them like that. They were just my youngers, but I never disrespected them. It made sense to give everyone ratings until they didn't deserve your ratings, that's the way I saw it. But I missed the olders for real.

In the Second year, I got to know the man that had made it through the First year, better, even if we weren't in the same class. We started to chill on our breaks, playing basketball, chess and blackjack. Michael Jordan was the man back then and we all wished we balled like him, so when Big T arranged basketball at a leisure centre in Higham Park after school on Mondays, we were on it. Aunty, Johnathon and them's mum worked there. I always asked her how they were, she always said,'They cool.' Time had passed, but we were all still on the endz, so I knew I'd catch up with them again soon.

Bare man went training on that Monday night. Some heavy ballers played there still. I have to admit, I weren't ready. Even my brother played there certain times. This one night we there playing and I'm getting checked out the sky by everyone, it weren't even just the olders. Obviously, I weren't feeling that. Who would like getting checked like that? It's like, they were trying to make me nervous even shooting, it was that bad. I'm thinking *fuck this you guys better take me more serious*, so as I went in for another layup, one man came in on me with another hard check. But this time, I brought my arm down heavy on his nose. My man screamed like fuck that evening cause I broke his nose clean. Everyone in school heard the next day and wondered if I done it on purpose. I just left them to wonder, but after that, they played a little more cautious around me.

After that (and now Langer had got kicked out) I was looking alright as a baller. I had man like Lindon who was totally shit, making me look half decent too. He was so bad, when I watched him play, I thought *even all this practice ain't gonna help this guy.* Man like Langer though, he was the best in our school from he reached as a first year. My man was tall and dunking already. He was always getting kicked out, he looked like a terrorist. He was taller than all the teachers and some of them would have been shook to death just looking at him.

But yeah, Lindon loved basketball, maybe more than me. The funny thing was, he actually thought he was alright. Man couldn't tell Lindon he was shit. He used to chill with me on Mondays before basketball in the evening, then he'd get a bus from my yard, or go chill with Pauly one of his bredrins for the evening, if he didn't find another way to get home.

Lindon had tings hard - I think it was the same kind of set up for him like it was for me - we wanted to be out of the house as long as possible. We had a court in my local Priory Court estate too and us man would play for hours in all kind of weather. Certain times we played till we could barely see the ball.

He lived in Stratford, miles from our school. His dad never gave him enough money to eat and catch bus both ways. One apple for the day was harsh! Me and O'Neil felt bad for him certain times, so if we had it, we'd give him our change so he could get the bus home. If we didn't he'd have to walk all the way or link Pauly if he was staying with his dad round the corner from me. Pauly was blessed still when I got to know him, he should have come our school.

It stayed routine in school for that year, with us man controlling the ting until summer came and we were leaving that site about to get upgraded.

SUMMER 1992

LEAVING FOR
SUMMER HOLIDAYS

CHAPTER SIXTEEN

It was summer time again and I had a feeling this summer was gonna be crazy. It was the first summer my cousins Andrew and Mark from Toronto where coming to stay for the six-week holiday. Andrew was the same age as me and Mark was a few years younger. All we had to worry about was looking fresh and not losing no stripes. It was my responsibility to make sure they were nice and show them wha gwan on the endz. I was growing up to be a proud-of-myself yute, trust me. Fuck them teachers and what they said, I didn't believe them. They was out here trying to imply I was gonna be a failure.

From Andrew landed, he loved how tings was popping. Tru Mark was a few years younger, he didn't roll with us that much, on the man dem ting. But Andrew, he was rollin and feeling how the crew was big. We'd play basketball in the Priory Court Estate, morning time, before the day got started. Sometimes we'd go out with Mumsy to the Science Museum or somewhere like that, but more time, we'd go out with the man dem. I didn't like going out with Mumsy anyway, I felt like she always tried to embarrass me on purpose. One time we were in West End going to see Big Ben.

We got on the bus and me, Andrew and Mark went up-stairs; Mumsy stayed downstairs. When it was time for us to get off, Mumsy sung my name out like she's der in the opera. I tried to act like she weren't calling me, but that's the kind of thing she done on a regular.

I think for my cousins, staying here was as much fun as it was for me, them being here. My yard was similar to where they lived and we were on the same kind of tings. I had a new girl all now too, Tammie. I was still shy, I guess that was because me and my Mum hadn't really talked since my Dad left and G had knocked my confidence, but I was getting there and her cousin Claudia rolled with her when she came to look for us. Justin was on her, but they weren't together like that. I was still surprised though when I see Andrew and Claudia finding things to do when I was half feeling up Tammie. *Wink Wink*

I brought him in nice and I could tell he didn't want to leave when his holidays was coming to an end. I didn't want him to leave either, cause tings were just warming up, but Nottinghill Carnival was the last big event of the summer – sorting out garms and shit so we looked fresh, lining up after parties to touch, tru we were feeling like VIPs. It was a lot back then. We had done all the all-dayers there was, but because of all the beef there was the year before, they didn't put on as many the year my cousins came; but the weather was still nice so everyting was still all good. No school and that!

A few days before carnival me and the man dem decided to go try get some garms in some designer warehouse off the endz. I thought I'd bring Andrew along to try a ting, *I weren't really thinking*. We travelled all the way to Enfield on the bus. Got to the spot and split up looking real bait. I picked up what I wanted, hid the shit and went to the changing rooms. They gave me a ticket for three items when I had seven. I ripped off the alarm tags and pushed them up my top, lucky for me I moved slower than some of the others. The establishment knew exactly what we were in there doing, so they called the boy dem.

Me and Andrew saw them as they pulled up out front. If the boy dem were smart, they would have waited round the corner and caught all of us on the way out, but they weren't. I walked around the store till I found the best place to drop the shit. I found a spot, then strolled out like I *was* nice. I was nice! They pulled us instantly and started searching. They could search me, I was cool. Del weren't, not that day! Everyone see them pull up out front except Del, so when he came out, he got sucked off (arrested) for the rest of that lovely summer's day. His mum had to go pick him up from the boy dem station. I would have been pissed. My mum would have had a heart attack, or she'd have sent my brother, or both, and I didn't want either.

CARNIVAL BACK
IN THE DAY

CHAPTER SEVENTEEN

Carnival got started for us on the Saturday at Panorama. You could smell Carnival in the air from King's Cross. People bubbling, vibing nice with their costumes, chicks looking sexy and shit. Us man got there about seven that evening. Man was setting up equipment in Ladbroke Grove, testing their sound systems and shit. Ladbroke Grove was cracking over that weekend, always. Everyting was looking nice, but we didn't stay long tru we were hitting one dance we had VIPs for. All we had to do now was holla and us man were in on the guest list. We hit the club that evening and skanked till early morning, then jumped on the bus back to the endz. Sunday was family day at Carnival, that's why it weren't a big deal us getting there late. And this is back in the day when Carnival was proper. Carnival would done all three, four o'clock in the morning. We didn't wake up till about midday, raving with Wisdom, getting fucked up on the rum and black, so we got to Carnival about three that afternoon. It was always nice to see people at least try hold it down on family day, but you would still see the helicopters directing the boy dem to where the beef was kicking off. Rampage was always the first spot we touched. That's where everyone links up; if you had beef or you were looking beef, that's where you'll more time find it. Rampage was the sound us man had been following from morning, Rosemary days. Their sound controlled a road on their own, they were that big.

We linked some of the man there and saw some beef kick off, then the road got gassed, so we left for a bit. As we were leaving, in the mayhem, a guy dropped his phone; he smashed his bottle on the floor for glass too fly all over the place on people. That kicked off another beef, cause man weren't having it. But the Sunday was a nice warm up and none of us got into anything serious, so it was a good day.

Monday come and I wondered *what's gonna happen today*, all the tugs came out on Monday, so to be in Carnival all day and nothing happen was highly unlikely, but man stayed optimistic tru it would have been nice. We rolled out with a hangover from the night before, getting fucked up again, standard! We got there, me, my cousin, Oki, Justin, Squeaks, Jups, Bigger, Nats, Del, Toks, Abbs and Play and linked man like Baby D, J Makaby and the rest of the man dem at Rampage, then we done the rounds. We had a little look at Westwood and some other sounds. All I could say was *Bare Gyal*, all over the place! Man and man were in the element when chicks was deh bout, looking all sexy and showing man love. All this time we taking numbers, making links for winter, cause it was coming and fast. Back then I always wondered why they made it the last week of the holidays. There wouldn't have been half the trouble there was in the summer, if they put it at the beginning, because the chicks we linked in Carnival would have kept man cool and holding it down for the rest of the summer. But as I got older, I got to find out they didn't want beef to stop. *If there was no beef, the boy dem couldn't justify the year on year inflation in the budget.*

We done well staying together though so long. The whole

day we managed to stay about forty man strong, linking more man along the way, drawing more chicks. Then 7 pm came and the sounds had to start turning off their shit. We left Rampage and started walking up the hill towards Westbourne Park station. Man started running through the crowd, like everyone's gonna be able to stick together in all them people. It was Abbs that started the running ting, racing through the crowd, bouncing guys and pissing people off. We got split up into groups of between five and ten and after a while it was long trying to find man in all that. It was my cousin I was worried about, I couldn't take him Carnival and lose him, but that's exactly what happened.We just figured we'd link man at the top of Westbourne Park Road. When we got to the top we found them. I was hoping my cousin was with someone. He was, *thank fuck*. When we linked up, he told me someone had troubled him and he knew where he was, so we all went and linked that brea. Man were too strong for him and his crew on the day, my cuz roughed him up and that was that, but the brea was serious. We didn't know who he was at the time, but a few months later we found out.

After that little politics, we got back to the Carnival spirit and found a live float to follow and carried on chasing floats till about four in the morning. It was all good though, cause the fun weren't finished. We still had that journey back to the endz. From Carnival to Trafalgar Square, then home. We couldn't hit no dance cause mans dough (money) was done, but we didn't need dance. We'd danced enough tarass, we was just pissed it had to come to an end.

Carnival was the end of summer - it was the last bit of fun we'd have before going back to school. And on the Tuesday, my cousins started getting ready to go home too. I wished they could stay. The day before they left we went out to take pictures with the man dem. I was too big to cry, but it was emotional. We went to the airport with them. I knew Andrew had had a big time and he was feeling real, flying home in his new red Versaces, but he was still pissed he was leaving so soon.

When they left, everything went back to normal and I got ready for school, some of the man dem were starting college that year, so man weren't gonna be seeing them as much either and there were a few new man dem rolling: Shit was changing!

HUMBLED –
I HAD THINGS TO SEE
AND PEOPLE TO DO

CHAPTER EIGHTEEN

After that summer though, we got upgraded to the old block, back with the olders. It was nuts how, from they turned Fourth-years, it's like they were running the school. Being at the old block now, it was easier for me to go Central and catch the W11 back to my yard. And Mark's was on the way towards Central. Mark's was the arcade just before Central, where we used to play Street Fighter till our money ran out. Green School was a girls' school along the way and them girls were feeling us Holy family man.

A lot could happen in that stroll down to Central from the old site. So when my year moved to the old site, me rushing home to link man dem at McKenty was long. I had things to see and people to do. It was more likely, man might link at Central, but I weren't rushing again.

One of them afternoons, as we walked down to Central from school, Preacher, one of my year olders came and asked: 'Yo Chris, you want to fuck one Green School chick?' I said, 'Course!' thinking he was joking.

When he showed me the chick - I said, 'Rah, is that what time it is?' *It was on! She was the same year as me and Preacher told me*, 'she's on it; she wants to take some cock'.

Now we had to find somewhere to beat. That was a mission, we was about to run battery on this chick, so comfortable yards weren't available, it weren't the kind of party where you can bring everyone home. We walked up and down for about an hour looking for somewhere, but man were calm cause we were all looking forward to what we were gonna get. It was cold though so we decided to take her to one abandoned house. The mission just to get there was crazy; we had to pass toxic waste, *a blatant health hazard*, climb up hill and cross gully. I didn't know a chick on the planet, other than her, that would have done all that willingly to have seven man, one after the other dig her out, but she was on it.

I was the number three in line, after Preacher and Bernett. When I check it, I did have ratings cause the olders waited and didn't complain. When it was my turn, Preacher gave me a dom and said, 'Here Chris, put this on!'

I couldn't tell man I was a virgin. I took it and said,'Cool!' My heart was beating all now when I got inside, I was nervous trying to act cool.

She told me, 'Come,' as she stood up with her legs open against the wall. This chick that was about to take my virginity was looking at me all now. There weren't no turning back, no time for excuses. I put on the condom fumbling all the way. I hadn't put a condom on before so I weren't even sure if I put it on right. I was under crazy pressure to, man and man were eyeballing the situation hard outside listening for noises and shit. It was dark and I didn't know what pussy felt like, so I was there for a while not sure if I was in. Then after a few strokes knowing I was in, I cum. As much as I tried to be cool, it was very clear I didn't have a clue what the fuck I was doing. But when I pulled out the condom was full so that was good and it was nice for me, *I weren't sure about her.*

Before the end of the week, the number of man that was

on her was crazy. She had man leaving school early, sneaking out of class to run battery, it was a lot. I fucked it once more at the time, before I felt like a scavenger, begging-pussy brea and left her alone. Losing my virginity to her under them circumstances was fucked though and to make it worse, after about a week she told the man dem I couldn't fuck. Tammie was my chick still at the time and obviously she was looking a beat too. I'd been with her a few months and now this chicks dissed me like this. She had me questioning myself again. On top of that she exposed my short-comings to man that couldn't wait to sing that fuckery from the school roof top. I came into school after they told me she told them, feeling like the joke. I was humbled for the week; she smashed my cool reputation to pieces with that talk. I was very embarrassed! I'll never forget that maths class, I came in a little late and see everyone looking at me funny. I don't know what Shelly thought, but, knowing she knew didn't sit well on my chest. It took me a while to shake that one off, but the reality was she didn't say I was small, she just said I couldn't fuck. So when man tried diss me, even though I didn't admit I was a virgin, man knew, so everything got back to normal kind of quickly and I shook that one off. The reality was, most of the man in my year hadn't even fucked yet, so they couldn't talk to me. All my booboo taught them was, don't lose your virginity to a douche bag.

FRIEND ZONE

CHAPTER NINETEEN

As well as that, Shelly, the girl I should have lost my virginity too was dealing with Abbs all now. They had started seeing each other that summer. Abbs had linked her with Jubs, when Jubs was dealing with Aisha, Shelly's niece. They had been going out for a few months, so it was a little uncomfortable. I started to see the potential in her too late and she changed her hairstyle to extensions. That was all she needed and now I was in the friend zone with her for life. It was cool though, I had learnt now that I didn't want– everyone knowing my business.

That situation with that Green School chick knocked my confidence a little though, I'm not gonna lie, so I started longing-off Tammie. I couldn't deal with the embarrassment again, especially so soon after that. I knew Tammie was cool, but she was a Totty chick and them chicks could hot a guy who didn't perform and that weren't gonna be me again. I thought, *let me chill off the gyal ting for a bit, and try get my money up with man dem.* I ended up telling her I need a little break but we still cool.

That Friday after me and Tammie finished, me and a few man were bored so we decided to touch Trocadero, see wha gwan. We met some West London chicks on the way talking about, 'we having a dance this evening in West and you lot should come.' We were on it, why not! It meant our week-end was gonna feel longer, so we left Trocadero about eleven and dialled her in to get the address. The dance was in the chick's yard about ten minutes' walk from Shepherd's Bush Central line station. We got there on the last train with no care how we were getting home. Rolling on this one, it was me, Oki, Dragon, Jups, Abbs and Play. This house party was jam for a Friday night, but with bare man. I'd say it was about ten man to two chicks up in there, but with us man, as long as there were available girls inside, we were cool. And there was a few spare for us man.

After about twenty minutes getting comfy and shit, who do we see, Marky and some of the older man dem. I was shocked to see them man, I can't lie. We were clean on the other side of London, so we in this dance all now, skanking, getting fucked up on brandy and cokes till someone broke her toilet. After that she stopped the dance and made every-one leave. I was having a good time, so I was a little pissed. But shit happens, so we said our byes and come outside.

Outside we hear shouting, 'GIVE ME THE TING!'; 'GIVE ME THE TING!'; 'LOOK WHAT HE DONE TO MY FACE!'; 'let me shoot that brea!'; 'LOOK WHAT HE DONE TO MY FACE!'

This guy had a wet from his eye right down to his chin. He was asking a next yute for his gun, so he could lick shots after the brea that done it. But his bredrin weren't having it, 'Nah blood', his bredrin told him. 'You can't use my ting!'

I could see shit could pop off any time in London at these random dances I was beginning to love. Seeing the olders get into their whips and roll out was emotional, it's tru the weather was bad, but it was all part of the fun. Us man trav-elled back to the endz on the bus.

The next day, I got up late and I was on my way to link

Oki when I see Kinger in the market. Kinger was one of my foundation man dem I had met at the Gamble's yard back in the day. He was a McKenty man. A hard-back yute still! I asked him, 'What you on'?

He said, 'You no me fam', that meant he weren't on nothing other than robbery really, if he got a chance.

So I told him, 'I'm going to link Oki, come innit'.

So now we walking towards Oki's. We der in the market and who do we see, that Green School chick.

I told Kinger, 'We can beat that ting ya know.'

He said, 'Don't lie, how you know that?'

I said, 'I beat it already with six other man'.

He said, 'Don't lie, line it up then cuz,' all excited.

I went over to her and said, 'Wha gwan, what you on?'

She said, 'Nothing, what you doing?' Even though she told man I couldn't fuck, she was on coming with us, I could see it. So I told her,'Come with us innit, we chilling. We gonna get some drink and watch movies at my bredrin's yard' She was on it, so we took her back to Kinger's yard, tru his parents were on holiday.

Kinger beat it first tru we was in his yard, then me. Even though I was new to the game I was feeling the feeling. We were on a bed all now too, so it was a lot more comfy, but I still didn't have a clue what the fuck I was doing and she told Kinger that too. I should have known she would and Kinger was never gonna keep that one quiet. Kinger brought in everyone else after that first link and within a week everyone I knew was digging it out. He told the rest of the man dem what she said too, so the man dem were giggling after me for a minute on that one. It done my street cred a little damage, all this, *'He can't fuck talk.'* I aint gonna lie. My reputation was important to me as a cocky yute, so something needed to happen.

LEARNING THE
HARD WAY

CHAPTER TWENTY

The year 1993 was a time where the man of my generation were reppin their endz with sounds systems. Our sound was Lexus. Jup's Dad and Mervin's Dad were big sound man from back in the day, so we had access to real artists and dub plates to kill sound boys. Hackney had Wisdom Hardcore and Black Mafia; Tottenham had Poison and Lady Force; Leytonstone had Power Love. We were cool with everyone except Power Love. Its tru it was between us and them for the spotlight in Waltham Forest at the time, so that's the reason we had politics. They were a little more rowdy than us, but we weren't dickheads and we had more gyal. On a real though, we shouldn't even have had beef with them man. There were school ties between us, but we were yutes with big egos. Shit was always gonna happen. We should have just clashed them and put them to bed with serious dub plates, *but we never did.*

The weekend was here and us man was on this Totty dance. It had a lot of hype around it cause Totty had bare gyal and Lady Force, Black Mafia, Poison and a few other big Hackney and Tottenham sounds were playing. I loved Totty for its girls. They had some of the sexiest girls in London right there, it's just that the attitude on some of them was stinking certain times.

We got there about twelve that night fully loaded. All of us had our one pops, borers and gas on us. We was in Totty, everyone in Totty carried something, so man had to be careful or bad shit could happen. Security was tight so we parked off our tings round the corner under some bins and went in. It weren't as serious as I thought it was gonna be, to be honest, but we knew bare man inside and the sounds were doing their ting still. We weren't trying to stay long, but about an hour after we reached something kicked off, so the management done the dance. That was a piss-take cause whatever happened really weren't that serious. Man started talking about we want our money back. The security weren't having it, so man was looking to gas it.

We went to get our tings, but someone had robbed us. They must have seen us put our tings down before we went in. I was pissed, I loved my one pop. Whoever see us put them down was happy to find all them weapons, *trust me.*

FAKE TOUGH GUY

CHAPTER TWENTY-ONE

Back in school on the Monday, certain teachers were getting new balls, feeling real out here, like Mr Bean. In the First year, this guy was the football coach's helper; by the time I was comfortable in the Third year, he was the headmaster. When he was the football helper guy he was cool; when he turned headmaster, he turned into a real dickhead. This Monday, lunchtimes finished, I'm on my way to my next class. This guy sees me in the hall way and stops me. He said, 'What have I told you about wearing blue suede shoes, boy?' In his thick Irish accent, as he stood on one of my shoes - like he's buying my shoes.

I snapped at him, 'You've got the wrong guy and don't stand on my shoes! Are you buying my shoes?'

He was trying to mug me off, so he asked me, 'Are you giving me back talk, boy?'

I told him, 'Yes, DON'T STAND ON MY SHOES.'

He said, 'Well, don't wear them then, boy,' as he walked off.

Pussy Hole!

With dickheads like that, you can imagine how I loved my weekends. We always had something to do. If we weren't touching South or somewhere going to link the Tro-cadero links we made, we were hitting a dance somewhere. Mumsy didn't even ask me where I was going anymore and my brother had gone missing again, so he weren't saying nothing.

The only thing that changed around the time really… was money started becoming an issue. The pocket money Mumsy was giving weren't making it. Trocadero and Street Fighter needed money, all the partying and drinks needed money. Our parents didn't have no Common Law Trusts setup for us, so we could hide our income and live like the elitists did. The poorest people paid the most tax, while the richest hid their assets in Trust and laughed at us. I didn't know all that then - but what I did know was me and my crew needed to EAT. Man like Oki came up with our first EAT. It was the launderette scam! It didn't need much brains, but we were young and it worked. Oki worked out how to open the money tray without anyone noticing. It was the same ting for a few in the area and we paid atten-tion to detail; that's why it lasted so long. We wouldn't take all the money and we waited a few days before the owners came for their month's takings before we hit them. I was the lookout guy. Anytime someone came, I'd stamp my foot like I'm dancing so Oki knew to put the shit back and sit down like we waiting on clothes. It was a nice little scam for Street Fighter money, but I needed more. No one taught me how to hustle. I wished someone did, we needed P's coming up in London.

NEW BARBER ON
THE ENDS

CHAPTER TWENTY-TWO

It was around the time Squeaks came to me one afternoon and asked me to cut his hair. I don't know what made him ask or even trust me, but I thought about how Sheriff had eaten likkle food over the years tru that. All Squeaks said was, 'Don't fuck me up like Martin done to Buju that time though.' We took time to giggle on that morning we linked up at Central the year before and everyone was crowded round Buju, one of our olders, waiting for the bus to take us to school. I wondered what was so funny with man's hair, cause everyone was asking him to take off the cap. Buju weren't taking off shit. Swift (another year older) sneaked up on him and dragged it off. Everyone started bussing up at him. Martin, the guy that cut it was there too laughing. He had cut the shape of a broken egg with jagged sharp bits all the way round Buju's head, even the front where the mark-up should have been. No fade! Buju got dissed for the whole day. The next day he was bald.

After I laughed till I almost wet myself, I trimmed Squeaks in a classroom with some clippers he brought. Squeaks was feeling the trim too, so he went into the playground and told everyone I done it. From then, I was the barber in school. Sheriff had a long queue on the weekends and man had got tired of waiting for him. So, within that week I had a little queue starting with Merv and O'Neil that were waiting on me. Then Chopper asked me to cut his hair in his yard in Totty. I didn't have clippers, so we went and linked a few of his man dem looking for some, Wang Wang ended up having the clippers. Wang Wang was Dragon's cousin, but I didn't know that at the time. Back then he was a big name, known for madness. He was bad before a lot of man was bad and everywhere he went something popped off. I ended up trimming both of them that evening at Wang Wang's yard. And after that, I was the next barber on the endz.

FIX UP

CHAPTER TWENTY-THREE

I had love for Totty man, they were going on with tings.
Ratty was another Totty man that had started our school
that year, as a Forth year. He came from the same part as
Chopper and he knew man like Gansta and Newancy who
had started in McKenty. Ratty was key man dem from he
reached our school, he was a joker. Man and man would
chill on breaks and travel to Central from school, where
we'd get caught in Mark's for hours playing Street Fighter. I
remember the day he came into school after smoking weed
for the first time. We linked at Central in the morning, then,
walking to school he started telling me about the day before. He said, 'I was fucked Chris and my head was spin-
ning, I weren't sure if I was ever gonna be cool again!' We
giggled about it on the way.

When we got to school, man was giggling hard as I linked
Squeaks. Squeaks, was on other tings though, talking about
this American chick, Lajoyce. She had moved to London
with her family from States, so now she was going secondary school here. Squeaks told me he saw her on the bus. She
didn't go to our school, but, because she went Tom Hood,
she had to get the W16 bus and that passed our school.

Squeaks used to see her in the morning when she passed on the bus.

He told me 'she's sexy, from you see her, you'll know it's her.' I liked the sound of that, so I was looking out. It took a few days, but when I saw her, Squeaks was right, I knew it was her. I went over and had a word and she gave me her number. I was feeling her, so I was trying to be that gentleman. I would wait for her at the bus stop in all kind of weather. Travel some of the way to her house with her, breddin (*kissing ass*) and talking a lot of shit along the way. I was actually putting myself out travelling that way to go home. I wanted her to see the nice guy in me and excuse my short comings. Its tru fucking was a touchy subject after my little situation. I did fuck it after we started dealing though. But it was another disaster, so I had mugged myself off again, after all my attempts at being nice. Obviously, I had learnt certain things from that Green School chick so no one found out about that one.

After Lajoyce, I stopped that nice guy shit, waiting by bus stops for chicks. *I needed to fix up!* All the women in my life so far had shown me no moral support or loyalty. I thought, *why the fuck should I keep trusting these chicks to care about my feelings. If they don't care about mine, why the fuck should I care about theirs.* This was the first conscious decision to change that I made, *fuck them* that's how I saw it!

OBVIOUSLY

CHAPTER TWENTY-FOUR

The first chick after Lajoyce I fucked was Natalie, one of Merv's link's bredrins. Merv was the guy in my year that wore the trainers too big for his feet. Tru we lived round the corner from each other, we had started travelling home together certain times. I hadn't rated him in the beginning, I ain't gonna lie, but he was a gyalis (sweet boy). His tings name was Reds, so when he linked her and she brought her bredrin, the bredrin was for me and Natalie, she was decent. She was a slim ting from Manchester, dark skin and cute in the face, but on this rude gyal ting. She thought she was hard in the beginning. Reds was trying to have up Merv, so Natalie must have thought she could try the same ting with me, but I weren't having none of it.

I changed up everything with Natalie. My encounters with these chicks so far had taught me enough, so I knew the basics. I took time with her and I realised then, that, when you give good cock, you could take the bass out of their voice and I liked that. She behaved herself quickly after I proved myself, sucking my cock nicely too and I remembered thinking… *I ain't gonna have no more problems with these chicks.* How wrong could I have been!

Obviously, now I've got this chick massaging my ego, my confidence with these chicks slowly came back. Tru she was a traveler - back and forth from Manchester - where she came from and High Wycombe where she was studying. I didn't see her as much as I would have liked. So, while she was away, now I was a little more confident with my stroke, I looked out for other chicks to help pass the time. Other yutes had learnt watching porno's, I hadn't, so I was playing catch-up, but I was catching up.

The first random chick I drawed to pass the time was Leana, she was really fucking random. She seemed a little slow too, but she had ass and titties with a decent face. After a little small talk I asked, 'What you doing later?'

I was cheeky so I gave her giggles and tru she was feeling me, she said,'Nothing.'

I told her,'Come look for me later innit.'

I had to sneak her in, cause Mumsy was going on bad. And I kept her sneaked in till morning. She took body three times that night and before she left. Her pussy was sweet and she soaked all over me, she rocked the mic nice too, to round off a lovely evening. I was feeling real as I sneaked her out clean. Mumsy didn't even notice that one.

Bonita was next. I troubled her coming back from one fireworks display in Hackney. I was feeling her submissive soft whisper that screamed *fuck me* at the same time. It was weird! We spoke after I smiled and said,'Wha gwan.' She was from Edmonton visiting her grandma in Dalston.

She gave me her number and told me,'Holla.'

She was fucking right I was gonna holla. I holla'd that same evening on the new basher (phone) Merv got me on one of his fraud moves. I talked to her for hours that night on my Mercury One2One. Mobiles were keeping us man connected now, so there was no need to rely on the house phone again. She oozed sex appeal, that voice hypnotised me. She had me a little weak from the start, but she was feeling me as well, so we made arrangements to link a few days later. The beat weren't as good as the verbal four-play, but Bonita was cool. I was pissed when we lost numbers cause my basher got cut off so I lost all my contacts. She moved same time, so I couldn't link her and I couldn't knock her grandma's door. *NO WAY!*

Sharon was the next ting after Bonita. One West London chick, I was with Squeaks and Merv when we linked them and Squeaks drew her bredrin. Merv drew Lyiah, Squeaks tings sister, but 'Facety' ended up taking that.

These where a few of the chicks I was fucking with while Natalie weren't around. But there actually were quite a few others and I realised me and Natalie weren't gonna last, so it didn't take long before we were curtains. She weren't on the endz much and I did visit her once or twice in her uni town, but that was long. I definitely had love for her, she had brought me back. I guess because of that I didn't want to hurt her. I was starting to understanding the game and how it went. And as my confidence grew, I started loving those meaningless one night stands. As I fucked these random chicks, I felt a love I never had. The emptiness I had felt for so many years was being replaced with a neediness from these chicks – I was never gonna take the time to get to know.

WHO'S GOING ON WITH TINGS?

CHAPTER TWENTY-FIVE

By the Forth year, Merv was going on with a few tings still, apart from the fact he had got me my first basher. He could make certain tings happen, so I started letting him come on certain moves with us. He had a brother name Castro that I brought in too. Castro came from South; Pretty Boy we called him, tru he was a coolie with the waves and shit. Him and Merv weren't real brothers, but they had the same sister so they were family. Castro had a likkle edge on Merv though, especially after I started fading him out. His mum decided to put him in a different school to us, but in the evenings and on the weekends he was rolling.

By now, me and the crew thought we were big. We thought we knew it all. Mumsy couldn't really tell me nothing again. She had tried to give me a beating with the belt for coming in late one evening and it was so funny I laughed. My brother had found another chick so he bounced again to go live with her. I was back to doing what I wanted, when I wanted to. Mumsy should have tried something new, but she was getting old and didn't have the energy anymore. She didn't know what to do with me, so she left me to do what I was doing. She didn't like how I was living, but she didn't have any advice for me that made sense. And reminding me whenever she could, *'You going to be just like your worthless nigga father'* wasn't helping.

Mumsy had brought me up well, but she couldn't see, she made me feel like I was the worst yute on the planet. When I reminded her what was going on, out on road, she told me 'I don't care.' She should have, I was learning more from them than her. She was in a bubble, and what the yutes were going on with on road, she didn't have a clue about.

TALK OF THE TOWN

CHAPTER TWENTY-SIX

It was the summer again all now and it was almost time for the olders to leave Holy Family for good. This was the one time in the year, all the schools on the endz linked up at Walthamstow Pool and Track for sports day. Earlier that year, one of the top Leytonstone man had been rushed by some Totty man. Gansta and Newancy were on the endz, reppin McKenty; and Ratty and Chopper were reppin Holy Family. Tru they were Totty man, I'm surprised they even touched down on sports day that year, but they did. Leytonstone man were looking to fuck them up. The day was nice, real hot and everyone was there. No one cared about the sports today though, word on road was, Leytonstone man were coming. I was interested to see what was gonna happen. When I see them man come walking up the path towards the track, about one hundred and fifty man strong, Manny leading the way. Where I was standing was perfect to see wha gwan. Gansta was standing on a little hill, him one, getting changed when Manny see him. I looked at Gansta's face, he was not shook at all.

Manny said, 'Come outside Gansta, you and anyone you're with.'

I had to big up Gansta. He said, 'What the fuck are all the rest of you doing here, are you gay? Manny's the only one of you man who should be here right now!'

Tru we had that rivalry with Leytonstone, we were with Totty.

I told one McKenty man, 'Go find Newancy.'

Gansta said to them as they let him walk off, 'I'm going to get my man dem and I'm coming back!'

I was surprised cause Leytonstone had all their man there, if this was a Totty promotion, Leytonstone man wouldn't have been going nowhere.

Gansta and Newancy left and within forty minutes they were back. They didn't come back with bare man either. They came back with about eight man, just the Poison sound man dem, including a few of their olders. There was so many Leytonstone man, it was mad.

Then Totty man sat down on the kerb and told man,'Whenever you pussies are ready man's here, do what you're doing now or don't even look at us man again.'

By now, Leytonstone man numbers were crazy. The road was jam and Leytonstone man did nothing while Totty man walked up and down chilling, taking the piss, earning ratings and bare stripes. That was the talk of the town that summer. Name brand Leytonstone man on the endz were saying nothing. I don't know what happened before, but nothing happened then and a lot of man were watching. The ting was, Manny could scuff, but when shit hit the fan – he weren't sure who was really gonna back him.

That was the last major event before the olders left. The day they left the school, it should have been us man running them out, but it was them giving some of my year one final beating. I was one of the few man that never got it, a lot of guys did though. Some teachers got it too, eggs and flour all of them got. Two teachers got a beating, one got his head open by Johnny P with a crowbar. Man peeled back him bald head, Johnny P didn't go our school but he was man dem, so it counted. The other teacher just got rushed.

BACK TO CANADA

CHAPTER TWENTY-SEVEN

That summer I went Canada to see my cousins, Andrew, Mark and Chris. Chris hadn't been London yet; he was a few years older than us, but a few years younger than my brother. Tru my brother weren't around, it didn't make sense Chris coming cause he might have been bored. I had a lot to tell Andrew in the year I hadn't seen him. I told him 'Justin's pissed with you for doing a ting with his chick'– as he called her – Justin found out somehow and told me to say, 'He's gonna fuck you up.'

He was joking, but I told him anyway. Then there was the situation with that guy, man had roughed up for him in Carnival. It turned out he was a Junction man and in one dance Jups had been in over South, the guy had recognised him. Jups was outnumbered like he was at Carnival and they had smashed a bottle over his head and tried to bore him up. They were trying to take him outside too, but Jups weren't having it, he had to wait for all of them to leave. He looked out at them through the window, waiting. Jups was always fat, so running weren't something he liked to do, but he needed to run. It was a house party and he told the homeowner, 'I'm not leaving out the front, so if there ain't another way out I'm staying.'

They let him go out the back and Jups was on his toes. It weren't funny cause it could have been serious, so man took time to reflect.

ALL GOOD THINGS
COME TO AN END

CHAPTER TWENTY-EIGHT

Toronto was moving back then. It was clean, tidy and everyone was cool. I felt the love from my Aunt and cousins, like that's where I was supposed to live. The summers were long and nice which was perfect for me and there was always something to do. We would take out the bikes and go riding over G-Ross Park if Aunt hadn't planned something for us to do. G-Ross Park was just across the road from Aunt's yard, full with windy dirt track hills. These dirt tracks were crazy to ride up, then race down, but you had to be careful, you could get fucked up on them hills. We'd been racing up and down all day, there was this one dirt track that me and Andrew wanted to handle better. It was a serious hill and speeding down this one, you had to be a serious rider. We speeding all now, just about to take a sharp right but I didn't get low enough. I was a G on a bike tru my Dad's teaching methods, so I thought I could manage that corner at that speed, but I couldn't. I got thrown into the trees. I was lucky cause the trees broke my fall! It hurt my pride more than anything, but I got a wet (cut) too. As I walked the bike back to Aunt's looking at my wet, I thought *I'm not telling the man dem I fell off a fucking bike.*

Science Museum was another must, it seemed like in a summer holiday we had to do that as part of our family bonding. I remember none of us wanted to go with Aunt on this particular day, but tru she had arranged it already, we were going. It was downtown and Aunt was driving, so it weren't a big deal. It's just that there was bare tings to do just outside Aunt's yard, or even in the yard. Anyway, their Science Museum weren't shit, so man was enjoying the day.

I didn't pay it any attention at first, when, a few hours in I heard someone shout,'Chris!' I'm in Canada…who the fuck would I know here? *I thought.* I heard, 'Chris, is that you?'

I turned round to see Josh from school staring at me. I couldn't believe it: Josh, in the Canadian Science Museum same time as me. My Aunt and cousins were shocked as well, but being as cool as I thought I was, I played like it was nothing as we talked for a while. He had left my school in the second year so I hadn't seen him in about two years. *The world is small* I thought and trust me it was gonna get smaller.

While I was there I visited The CN tower, I watched an American football game in the only opening dome (at that time) in the world. And a few other things, but just chilling for the summer in Canada was massive. I used to think six weeks, that's a nice holiday, but it always went so quick. I didn't want to go home yet; I missed the man dem, but quality of life in Canada was much better. All good things come to an end though and my holiday was over, so it was back to the block for me.

WHAT YOU GONNA
DO ABOUT IT?

CHAPTER TWENTY-NINE

Back in school we - Fifth year now, we controlling shit. It's still the same crew but now the pipsqueak First years are grown and going on with tings. When our olders left, school was never the same. By now, a few of the guys that I didn't have ratings for had come up a little in the ranks. We were rolling in school and a little out of school cause I was trimming a few of them now still.

Third years I didn't notice other than Jamma (Justin's brother); Spray and T.The most memorable thing that happened in Fifth year was Shelly and Aisha banging up Joy and her mum. Joy was a Third year at the time and sexy, even back then, she was one of three girls in that year worth remembering. Obviously, I didn't get involved in Third year tings, so I didn't know exactly what was going on, but, I knew they had a problem. I think Aisha bullied Joy, tru she was pretty; so, one day Joy thought it would be a good idea to bring her mum down to the school. Her mum didn't look too big by the time that finished.

She walked straight up to the playground, where she knew Aisha would be, when she found her, she started shouting at her.

'YOU LEAVE MY DAUGHTER ALONE, YOU HEAR ME!

If I have to come back here again to tell you, you're going to be in BIG TROUBLE!' Shelly saw what was going on and went over, saying

'DON'T TALK TO MY NIECE LIKE THAT,'

then punched her in the mouth. She knocked her to the floor, then started dragging out her weave, scraping her back and kneecaps on the concrete same time. Aisha jumped on Joy…it was on, mother and daughter getting a beating in the playground for everyone to see. It was painful to watch. If I was Joy, I would have never come back.

After the beating, *then* her mum wants to go to teachers talking about what's been happening, as she's fixing her weave. I never saw Joy's mum at school again after that; the embarrassment must have almost killed her.

At home all now, my brother was back; he'd been seeing Dad. He told me, 'Dad wants to see you.' Dad was living in Leytonstone and I wanted to see him too still, it had been a long time, so one evening I went with my brother. I remember hiding behind his door, my brother suggested we surprise him. He opened up and my brother walked in with me behind. My Dad was living on the first floor of a one-bedroom flat all now, so we walked upstairs and followed him into the front room. He started talking, then he saw me. He couldn't believe his eyes, me standing there after all those years. It had been about seven years. I must have changed a lot since the last time he saw me. He had changed a lot too. It was good to see him, I can't lie and now I was old enough to make my own decision on what he was like. We talked for a while, then me and Andrew left.

School was coming to an end for us all now and I remember we were getting ready to leave. Dem same pipsqueak

First years had turned into some bad boys and they had more man than we did in my year. They had beaten us in basketball that last year, so they had grown to believe they could manage us, or at least some of us. They were actually telling some man, *don't bother coming school on the last day cause your whole year's getting run out.* The cheeky little bastards actually tried; furthermore, they actually did run out a few man never to come back, but me, Squeaks, Clay and T weren't running nowhere. Our stripes had been earned, enough to leave with nothing except the beating *we* gave the extra brave ones that thought about it.

I was feeling real all now. Leaving school for good and shit! I saw nothing but opportunities. I was finally free, or so I thought. Summer holidays were back and this was due to be a big summer, even though that little scam me and Oki were doing to get money had stopped. They had worked out what we were doing and tightened up security so the party was done. We were on the look-out for another scam and tru we were active in the community from North South East and West. We figured something would come up again soon. We always had somewhere to go or someone to link, mainly pleasure, but at the same time we were opportunists. This evening, early in the summer, me and Squeaks decided to go look for Leanne; tru she always complained we didn't make time for her. Her and her girls had been rolling with us man for a few years now. She was a Grove chick, one of many chicks we had linked in Trocadero. I knew she fancied me, but she was too much like man dem: loud, big and on this ting. There were times when she wanted to fight man with us. *We were in the friend zone for life!* But this evening, *tru we had time for her,* me and Squeaks thought we'd go look for her.

START SOME SHIT

CHAPTER THIRTY

We got off the Victoria line at King's Cross and got on the Hammersmith and City line going towards Grove. Our carriage was empty all now except for me, Squeaks, some skinny dark skin brea, who we sat quite near to and a businessman on the far side. Me and Squeaks were chilling, running joke and shit, as this skinny brea's watching us. I didn't think nothing of it, but I noticed. We were designered up from the garms (clothes) we had stole. We had been stealing designers for a while now. *This brea knew we were thieves from how we look - so we were fair game!* I had my chaps (gold bracelet) on too. When the guy see my chaps, he was on me. He got up quick and came asking, 'What area you from?'

I knew what time it was and even though I knew he was older than me, he was quite small. I thought, *this guy ain't-trying to rob me.* Then his bredrin came from nowhere. The Bredrin was some light skin brea, HENCH (big)! I didn't feel like I could manage him. The dark skin brea asked how old I was.

He told me, 'Stop lying,' when I told him, 'and take off that chaps.'

I said, 'Nah.'

He said, 'I don't want to bore you but I will, take it off!'
I said,'NO!'

Then he moved to take out his borer. He had plastic covering the handle. I wondered how many man he had bored with no prints on the weapon. Something about him said *serious*, I think it was the coldness in his eye.

I said, 'Here, look take it,' and gave him my chaps, *pissed*.

The next station was Grove, our stop; it was his stop too, so he told us to stay on the train. I couldn't even look at the brea as he got off. He knew, the businessman on the far side had more P's, I was just the easier target tru he knew I weren't going to the boy dem. Squeaks asked when they got off the train, 'How comes you said NO, then gave him your chaps?'

Tru he had his back to Squeaks, Squeaks didn't see his borer or the move he made for it.

After that, we didn't stop in Grove. I went home pissed. I was feeling my chaps and I wanted it back. That evening as I went to bed, something changed. *That weren't going to happen to me again and end like that.* I weren't a trouble-making yute, but I weren't having that again.

Squeaks said,'We should get the man dem and go look for them.'

I done already thought about that, but where would I start looking for this brea. I did want to start some shit, but I let it go. It was time to start becoming part of the solution within our community, not continuing the problem. *This is how easy it was for guys to get killed on the endz.*

EGO

CHAPTER THIRTY-ONE

It was the summer, Facety and his Leyton man became key man in my crew with Squeaks, Castro and Merv. The old crew split up when Oki moved to Beaumont Estate with his uncles. He kept everyone together as the barber, but he had stopped trimming on the endz so we didn't really link again like that, even though we were all still cool. Tru me, Castro and Merv lived round the corner from each other, certain moves we went on, it was just us until Castro went missing with one chick.

I was fucking one Peckham shorty at the time. I felt real fucking her, she always complained, 'You're hurting me Chris.' I thought that's what I was supposed to do. I was confused, but at least she weren't talking shit about I can't fuck. *She was another one massaging my ever growing ego.* I always had love for them South London chicks. Now we were getting older, we touched other spots too, like Liverpool Street Sunday market. It was live back then, man could steal and draw chicks too. One Sunday that summer, I remember me and Merv going, it was raining and cold and I weren't really on it. That's until I saw Sarah *my new wife.* She was so sweet, I was star-struck. I wouldn't normally talk to a chick with her mum right there and if I actually even saw her mum, I would have at least thought about not talking to her. But I didn't even see her mum. I could see the resemblance though, when Sarah introduced us. Merv drew Sheena the cousin; I think her mum liked me because she smiled and said,'Hello.'

Me and Sarah talked as we walked for a while, then she told me, 'I'll take your number.' I didn't like leaving them pretty chicks like that, but Merv got Sheena's, so that made me a little more confident. I used to give my number back then *and hope*; but I didn't like too, especially with the live ones. It was too fifty-fifty. But Sarah phoned me that evening and we talked like we knew each other for years. She was from West. I was feeling how she sexy; so even though it was far for me to link her with no whip, I was try-ing to make that effort.

My seventeenth birthday was coming and I was trying to work with this chick. I invited her to come chill with me for my birthday. Her and her cousin's birthdays were two days apart and in September like mine, just a few weeks before me. *Me and South, we were just fuck buddies.* It was all about Sarah. When she got down to mine though, it's like I could barely speak. This chick had me shy, but I had to ask her,'Would you deal with me, Sarah?'

She said,'Yes'.

I was happy.

So I'm seventeen all now, its 1995 and I'm feeling real. I can do my own ting if I get sucked off (arrested) by boy dem for some shit. That was a big deal. The last thing I wanted when I was going on with tings was to get sucked off and not be able to bail myself out, then have either Mumsy or my brother have to come get me. And now I'm dealing with Sarah, the baddest chick I've ever had.

A few days after my birthday, I was missing my chick, I wanted to go see her. Ear had lashed (stolen) a whip a few days before. He was one of the man dem from McKenty. Old school still! We called him Ear cause one of his ears stuck out. It was parked up on the endz. All it needed was petrol and we'd be rolling. Obviously, I'm using that car to go link the missus, so I told him, 'Come, let's go get it.' I told the Missus, 'I'm coming to look for you this evening ya na,' all excited. I don't know where that whip came from, I didn't give a shit, but some prick saw us fucking with it and called the boy dem straight. They were on us. I see them roll into the car park and froze like a dummy. I should have at least run, but we just let them get us. Ear had the bag, I was with him and we got sucked off on going equipped to steal and thief off the automobile. Boy dem always done shit. We were in Walthamstow, why the fuck would they take us to Chingford, when there's a station in Walthamstow? Other than to fuck with us, hoping we'd have to walk back and maybe get fucked up by some skinheads. They kept us in that station for eighteen hours as well. The first time I got sucked off, I'm getting eighteen hours detention. *Long!* I was pissed and I didn't know what to do. I weren't about to ask for help, so I just took what they was giving me and pleaded guilty. They gave me a caution for going equipped. When I got out, I holla'd Sarah, I said, 'The boy dem sucked us off on some bullshit, you know babes!' She didn't believe me at first, but when I linked her, I showed her the paperwork. I told Mumsy a story too cause I hadn't done that before either, stay out all night without telling her, Mumsy was cool though. It would have been different if she knew where I really spent that night, but she never found out.

All now, with these chicks, Merv was in a stronger position. Sheena loved him off so she would do anything for him. Sarah hardly ever came on her own to see me, like Sheena did. I didn't like the influence Merv had over my situation. He had say and I remember one evening Sarah phoned me to tell me, 'Merv's trying to set me up with a next man you know.' I said to myself, *Merv's trying to set up my missus with next man.* I had to ask him and he actually admitted it. He didn't get it when I was on the phone 'wiling out'. I had to go see the cunt for that. When I got to him, I said, 'Merv, Sarah's my girl, she's not a link or a chick we can share. I'm feeling her. What the fuck are you doing?'

I was pissed and he could see; he weren't sure what I was gonna do, so he punched me in the face and run off. I couldn't believe this fucker. I was so mad, I took a brea's crutch and chased him down the road. Tru he was one of the fastest in the borough at the time, there was no catching that bastard. He went missing for the next few days after that, then he made Sheena phone and talk it out for him. I knew he weren't thinking, he wouldn't try diss me on purpose. So after he finished breddin, I just told him,'Cool,' and lowed it. Me and Sarah weren't gonna last anyway, I could see it. I didn't know how to act with her. She took me back to my shy boyish nervous days. I left us to slip into the friend zone until we lost contact.

SERIOUS ALL NOW

CHAPTER THIRTY-TWO

All now man like Castro had been missing for a good while with his new chick he'd been seeing. It was the longest I'd seen him in a relationship and man was calling him a worm for bouncing like that. He was promoting this wifey ting hard. 'You should be settling down,' he was telling us, maybe to make himself feel better for how he had cut man off for this chick. We weren't watching that though, we was watching our money situation. It was getting serious now. I realised that summer, I needed a steady income. So I went looking a job.

Bobsy gave me one. He was one of the top old-school barber's on the endz. There was Darbie, Miers, Bobsy and Scalp him killer B. They worked in the same shop der in Hackney back in the day. They were the top barber's in East and everyone's mum sent their boy pickney (child) to one of them at some point. I weren't trying to be there all week like back in them days when them man controlled the ting. That was crazy! But Saturday and one or two days during the week could work. Bobsy was the man that taught me how to finish a trim, not the fade, Eddie and Oki taught me that; the cut-throat and the scissors, that was Bobsy. Diggie was the boss barber when I was there, he had the olders passing through. He was Garett from school's older brother. Dean was the other barber there with us. He was quiet but cool still. I could see he kept his thoughts close to his chest, kind of like me. Vinnie was like Bobsy's son, he would come and look for Bobsy almost every day.

When I started trimming there, after working all day Saturday, Trocadero was long. I was too tired for that shit and we'd had a madness in there so it was bait. Friday was my new Saturday and I had to finish up early because Saturday was an early start at the barber shop, so fucking new chicks became my main pastime.

The money I earnt at Bobsy's was ok for me as a yute, but I needed more. Living in London had my values all fucked up. Olders flossing on the endz looked strong and we were watching them man. So when that cell net scam started popping, it looked like the ting man had been waiting for. That network had been ripping everyone off for years, so when they brought out a mobile that could bash, everyone wanted one. Sim, brought me in, tru he had the link and I started shotting them, two-fifty a pop. When the phone was chipped, it would top back up each time you turned it off, back to ten pound. That scam lasted about six months and we ate well from it. It topped up the likkle money I made at Bobsy's and that gave man a little flexibility.

By now, me and my crew were established on the endz so when it came to chicks, I was feeling big in the game. I had even been accused of seducing one sexy chick who had a boyfriend. This chick was bad too. She had melted when I got her to my room and she was feeling what she got. When we finished, she said,'Chris, you seduced me.'

I'm thinking *what else would you expect from a 17-year-old 'man' going on with tings?* It was getting to the stage where I was wondering what was so different about settling down. Leon had been gone for a few months and he was looking like he was enjoying life.

The grass always looked greener on the other side. So when Jasmine came along, I decided to give this wifey ting a try. I met her in West End on one of those cold winter evenings when nothing special was going on. It was around Christmas time and everyone was out doing their Christmas shopping. This chick was sexy, browning with a cute face, about a size twelve with a size fourteen back-off! She had mastered this walk that talked without saying nutten.

I gave her my smile and asked, 'Yo you cool?'

She said, 'Yeah,'so we got talking, we running jokes and shit, getting on well then I asked her for her number. She weren't having it.

I told her straight, 'You know you're for me.'

I weren't trying to hear she weren't giving me her number, but I let her have mine in the end. I just made sure I saw her a few more times that evening. She was the one I was looking for or that's what I thought. *If I knew the madness she was going to cause I would have run far!* She phoned me the next day and we talked for hours.

The Monday after I met her, Justin went jail for armed robbery with S Yanks. This is how life had us. Junior told me when he see me knocking Justin's door. Junior lived a few doors down. He had gone my school too, he was just a few years older than me. He invited me into his yard and gave me some weed to smoke, as he told me what happened. He didn't know I didn't smoke weed and I didn't tell him. I was pissed to hear what happened to Justin so I felt like I needed some drugs. Justin was like a brother to me, I was gonna ask him what he thought about me settling down with this chick. Even though we didn't see each other every day anymore, his opinion still meant a lot.

DIDN'T KNOW SHIT

CHAPTER THIRTY-THREE

With Jasmine I thought I was ready. I'd had a few rela-
tionships, a few one-night stands and a few I could
barely remember. I was feeling like she couldn't teach me
nothing. She was a few years younger than me too, so in the
relationship, I was feeling cool, definitely in control. On top
of that I was proud of myself and where I stood amongst
my peers. She could see that as well!

Walthamstow was on the map all now tru E17, a little pop
group. They were big in England and Marky, my brother
and Donnie knew them man personally. It was good to see
them enjoying a little success tru they were bringing man
in. They were going strong about a year, then Donnie
formed a group, I remember seeing him on BBC 1. I thought
he must be making P's all now. It was good to see, even
though I hadn't seen him for years.

I was maturing all now and Jasmine was my steady girl,
things were even good with us in the beginning. That De-
cember when I met her, the nights were chilly and I wanted
her keeping me warm. She was bad (sexy) still, she made
herself well known to everybody around me too, but she
was Wifey, she could do that. The good things like that

back-off she had, had me overlooking her attitude. There was a big problem right under my nose that I weren't noticing… *them Totty chicks.*

I had been working in Bobsy's now for a few months and I had realised, cutting hair was never going to be my job for life. It didn't pay enough, so I decided I was gonna leave to go college. I had always intended to do that, but now I was in the shop, it reconfirmed what I thought. I had a little look around and decided, I was gonna go Westminster over South. Living in East and doing what we had done so far, East and North London had been rinsed. And things on the endz weren't even cool now, tru Popcorn one Totty man had been killed by some Hackney man. The endz got sticky after that cause someone always wanted to know where you come from and I didn't want to be around it.

And the boy dem were having us feel like, as long as we keep our murders directed at each other, investigations won't be intensive. And depending on the victim, the whole crime could just get swept under the carpet. They were using psychology on us, polluting our minds with tried-and-tested divide-and-conquer techniques. We didn't know that if we stood together as one unified people, No – One could fuck with us but yeah, It was fucked on the endz - I could see how things were going and what was gonna happen tru that. So I thought I'd come off the endz and be cool in South. I had heard a lot about this college too, so I wanted to see for myself what was really good. I saw this time in my life, not as time to be furthering my education, but more like a time to be meeting new people and getting more links, even though Jasmine was the Mrs and fucking other chicks couldn't really happen. I still liked to talk and I still wanted to just fuck around for a few more years, before I got that job in the music industry I wanted. *Wishful thinking!*

From school days, I believed I was a star and the world

needed me. It's a feeling the teachers worked hard to eradi-cate from us yutes that had that quality. *But what the fuck did they know?* Them hating just made me believe in my poten-tial more.

WE ALWAYS LEARNING

CHAPTER THIRTY-FOUR

On enrolment day, I signed up for the Health and Fitness course. In my class, I had man like Hard Back, he was from West; Andy was from Hackney; T from Highbury & Islington; Danny from Junction and sexy Karlene from South - she reminded me of Shelly from school days. Man dem in my class was cool, Danny knew some of the Junction man and so did Hard Back, but Hard Back weren't that cool with them. Karlene knew the Junction man too. Westminster was a Junction man's college. They had it locked. The first day I left class and took a look around, I was with Hard Back, T, Andy, Danny and Karlene. We walked into the common room and the entrance side was full with man. I didn't think much of it at the time, but I did notice. We found a seat and got something to eat, then chilled, but something weren't right.

After we ate, I got up to leave with the rest of the man in my class and one of the man controlling that side of the common room approached me. He said, 'Blood, I swear I know you from somewhere?'

I felt like I remembered him too, but I knew where this was going, so I said, 'Nah blood, I don't think I know you still!'

He said, 'Yeah, I'm sure I know your face.'

And that's when it clicked. He was the guy my cousin roughed up in Carnival and it was probably them same guys with him right there, that had bottled and rushed Jups trying to bore him up and had waited outside that house party in South, for him to come out. In my head I thought *shit, he's got a good memory.* By this time, his people noticed he was having a word, so they started coming over to see what was going on.

I said, 'Blood, I'm not from these endz and I don't remember you from nowhere.'

He was getting pissed cause he knew it was me, then Danny came over. He knew him so he said, 'Yo wha gwan?' to the both of us.

He explained that I was in his class and I'm cool, then they started talking about some other shit and that situation was dead. I ain't gonna lie, it was looking messy. If anything had kicked off on that first day, I would have had a problem in that college. Junction man were serious and I wouldn't have wanted that problem with them man on their block. I saw how they terrorised weak guys, but it was cool in there after that for me.

I stayed in Westminster for that year and started trimming Hard Back and the other T. Hard Back was about 6'4' and noticeable. Even though he was a West man, he had links in South. He knew them endz like I knew East and North. I asked him one day why he called himself Hard Back. He told me, 'I fell off the first floor of a building and landed on my back.' He didn't have any marks, other than one little graze he told me was a gunshot wound. So I wondered if he thought I believed him. Hard back was joker but bless still. The other T was cool too - he was more from my endz. He knew man like Moreno, Risky and the rest of them man from Highbury.

At the time, Merv went Highbury and Islington College. Sometimes I would go meet him and sometimes he would come meet me. Castro went Kingsway and Squeaks was rolling with Ratty and some other Tottenham man doing the ting. His mum had kicked him out, so he was staying back at his grandma's or at mine, if he weren't staying with one of his chicks'. Him and his mum had argued because Squeaks had stolen bare garms and tru his Mum hadn't bought them for him, she knew he had stolen them. Tru them garms were designers, they weren't cheap (even then) and his mum had ripped and burnt all of them. I knew he was pissed, he must have been. I remembered some of the shit he had done to get away after some of them moves. Waiting in ditches, jumping from mad high buildings, all kind of shit, but if his mum decided to burn his shit, what could he really tell her? Nothing!

Most of the old crew had gone Hammersmith and West London College, the livest college in West. Jups, Dragon, Abbs, Clayton, Bigger and a few others, but because they were older, they had left school a few years before me, so we were at different stages. We would still link up and use each other's college to link new chicks, visit other areas and just live the best we knew how, having as much fun as possible along the way but it weren't like the old days.

At the time, I was trying to be a good boyfriend. I was doing all the things couples did. We bought each other shit and I properly tried, but as we spent more time together, I started noticing the boo-boos, mainly possessiveness. Jasmine truly loved me to the bone, I could see that, but she was trying to tell me who and who I can go out with and a woman can't tell a big man them fuckery. I started feeling like this chick's a bit nuts and maybe this ain't such a good idea anymore. I felt I was too young for that shit. She wanted us to get married, do everything together and sometimes I just wanted to be with man dem or on my own.

So, coming up to the first year we'd been together I started wanting out.That's when she started acting up and I saw then that getting rid of Jasmine wouldn't be easy. She was friends with Lady Force, the big girl sound from Totty. They were well respected and I had love for most of them accept Rebecca.

LOOKING STRAIGHT BEEF

CHAPTER THIRTY-FIVE

To be honest, I had started loose-balling, talking to girls without caring and she was on to me so I told her, 'Look, I don't think it's working like this, we need to stop seeing each other as much.' She weren't having nothing like it though. So, she started meeting me places we didn't talk about meeting. At first, I saw the funny side and we giggled about it while I told her off. She'd say things like, 'Why can't your girl come and meet you Sibs, what you got to hide?' She was on a mission to catch me doing shit.

Ok, I was doing shit, but not much shit at first! Chicks like Bonita I'd lost contact with and found again, I had to go see, come on now. Especially now I had my first whip. Bonita had a baby now though, so after that first meet when she showed me her new place, I knew things were never gonna be the same, on top of Jasmine and her mad self. But as I was there, I thought I'd try a ting. But baby wasn't sleeping properly yet so I couldn't beat. And Jasmine was breathing down my neck too. In the hour or so I was chilling with Bonita, Jasmine called me about twenty times. She knew what time it was and always said, 'Just tell the truth Chris, I know you're fucking around. Just tell me, nothing's gonna happen. I just want you to tell me.'

I had told her some shit in pillow talk about,'I'll never hit you,' so she was feeling like she could do whatever she liked and she was onto me.

Tru I'd never been in a situation like this with anyone, I didn't know how to deal with what she was going on with. She didn't want to look like a fool, especially in front of her Lady Force girls. She felt I was fucking other chicks, so one evening when I was speaking to her on the phone, she thought she'd try catch me out. I was at Castro's - he had some chicks coming round, tru his missus weren't about.

Jasmine could sense I was trying to rush her off the phone. The chicks were supposed to be there already, so I'm there telling Jasmine, 'I'll be home soon, I'm just chatting to Castro for a bit then I'm coming.'

But something about my story Jasmine weren't feeling, so she said, 'Cool, I'll see you soon!'

Castro's mum was away on holiday, so it was just us in his yard. Five minutes later these chicks rang the bell. They decent, so now we all chilling in Castro's yard catching joke and everyting was nice for about twenty minutes.

When the door knocked the last person I thought it was gonna be was Jasmine, I didn't think nothing of it. Castro goes and opens the door, sees it's her and lets her in, like it's her yard. She marched in looking beef! My eye's opened wide, thinking *what the fuck are you doing here and why the fuck did Castro let you in?* The girls were shook to death.They didn't want nothing with her, the way she came in. That was the first madness I saw from her, she was embarrassing me. Got me out here look like a dickhead so I got serious and took her outside. She was going nuts, so I held her while she shouting at me and trying to scratch up my face. It was a lot, so to stop the madness I agreed to go home with her, back to my Mum's. I couldn't believe Castro let her fuck up the night. The girls left quickly after that and as they were leaving, they walked past us and told Jasmine, 'Nothing happened you know.'

Jasmine didn't give a shit, I was a cheat and she had caught me. She just went on and on about how I was cheating on her and that I should just admit it. Admitting stuff never got no one I knew anything other than booby prizes, so I weren't trying to do that. As time went on and weeks turned into months, she's playing the cheated-on house wife. She's staying at my house every day and not just because she had issues with her mum and her mum didn't want her to be with me (*her mum thought I was going to make her pregnant and destroy her life*). Jasmine knew, if she's at my yard, she can see what I'm doing even better. Mumsy liked her too, so she had half the battle won. So for me, all I could do was encourage her to go see her mum that was the only time I would have a break.

I remember things getting so bad one evening all because I wanted to go out on my own. She was not having it, accusing me of shit and telling me straight, 'I don't trust you Chris.'

I'd heard it all my life, first from Mumsy, now her. I didn't even care what she was saying. She was the new nagger in my life. I told her, 'Look, I'm going out with the man dem. I'll be back about ten thirty and when I get back, we gonna talk.'

I decided to go West with the man dem. Me, Squeaks, Facety, Castro and Dre. We had decided we gonna go link Sharon, Bonita, Lyiah and them West chicks. So I'm driving all now, we in Kilburn somewhere and I'm telling man dem how she's going on. We even giggling a little at the madness. Then I looked in my rear view and see this boy dem van driving erratic to catch me.

'Shit!' I said, 'It's boy dem and they on us.'

As they got behind me, they started flashing the headlights to see who was in the car.

When they realised it was a group of Black yutes, they blue-lighted and stopped us. I could see they was on us by the way they were driving, so I done already told man, 'Balls your tings' (hide stuff)

and I ballsed mine (weed) one of the man in my whip had hard food (crack). So I've stopped all now, they didn't give a shit about our names, they just got straight to the point.

'We can smell drugs where are they?'they said.

'We ain't got no drugs.'

'Stop with the fucking lies, just tell us where the drugs are.'

We said, 'Look, we ain't got nothing, you can check us.'

They said, 'You fucking right we will – we gonna strip search you in the van too.'

So they took us in the van one by one and strip searched us. When they finished, they stood us up against the wall, holding the weed and hard food. One of them pussy holes buss open one of the weed bags and gave a big *'ahhhhh'*, as he smelt it all happy and shit.

They smiled, then said, 'Right, now piss off.'

We were pissed cause we knew they were gonna smoke the weed and probably the hard food, it's the way the pussy smelt it and *'ahhhhh'd,'* we knew he was a smoker. If it was just weed, we would have told them, 'Nah, arrest us,' but because of the other stuff it was a little more serious, so we had to let that one go, a little more wise to these corrupt London pussy hole boy dem. To be honest, it shouldn't have surprised us. Where did all them racist skin heads go, them guys didn't just disappear. They were some of our Politicians, our Police, our Teachers, our Judges our Scientists our Dr's all out here still kicking us in the teeth.

DISRESPECT ALL NOW

CHAPTER THIRTY-SIX

We still went to link them West London chicks. But we didn't stay long, tru I still had this little problem that needed sorting with Jasmine. I was starting to have a lot of problems with her and how she was trying to treat Mumsy's yard. A few weeks earlier, she had come home late, trying so hard to creep she left the door open. I know she didn't mean to do it, but that was something I could use. I was looking any reason to tell her to get out all now. I was ready for her this evening, she had pissed me right off and then the boy dem done that. I got home about ten thirty expecting her to be there, waiting, but she weren't there coming on eleven.

She was taking the disrespect to a different level all now and I had to ask myself, *how far does she really want to take this, like I'm some funny guy.* I made up my mind, I'm kicking her arse out tonight. I was mad as I laid down in my bed waiting for her. Then, about eleven twenty, I heard what sounded like a car crash out on the main road. I remember saying, 'Them drivers are pissed,' then went back to waiting on Jasmine until I got a knock on my door. It was two boy dem, I looked out my window thinking it was Jasmine, wondering how comes she wasn't using her key and see them standing there. My mind went all over the place, thinking *why the fuck are they knocking my door. I didn't think they knew about anything I'd done, but I thought it's either I answer the door or Mumsy does*, so I put on my clothes quick and told Mumsy I'd get it, as I went to the door.

'What's the problem, officer?'

They said, 'Is your name Chris?'

'Yes!'

Then they said, 'Could you come with us please, there's been an accident with your girlfriend Jasmine.'

I said, 'Oh.'

Thinking i*t can't be serious if she told them where I live and it definitely can't be the crash I just heard.* I asked, 'What happened?' as I put on my shoes.

They said, 'We knocked her down as she was crossing the road.'

Damn, I thought as I looked at these pussy. As I got closer, I saw someone with a blanket on and her back to me, kneeling. I thought *oh, it's not that bad*, then I got closer and see Jasmine sprawled out on the floor, blood everywhere. It was fucked. She woke up just as I got to her and held her hand. I was mad with her before, but now, the anger went as I knelt and cried with her. She was in shock all now.

She said, 'Chris, I'm sorry for coming home late, I was with my Mum, talking.' Then she asked me how she looked.

I told her, 'Beautiful as always, babes.'

She said, 'Stop lying Chris, you don't love me now the police have knocked me down do you.'Then, as she finished saying that, she realised the boy dem had knocked out her teeth.

She screamed, 'CHRIS! I've got no teeth, where the fuck are my teeth?'

Then I looked on the floor where she was laying and see

four of her teeth lying there next to her. She fainted again tru the shock. She came back round in the ambulance travelling to the hospital. She kept asking me if she looked ugly and *where her teeth were?*

I told her, 'The doctors got them and said they gonna put your teeth back in, in hospital.'

She stayed in the hospital about five days after that and everything went well. The only problem the doctors said was, her teeth would fall out later on in life. Other than that, she'll be fine. When she got back home, I asked her what really happened.

She told me, 'I got off the bus, walked out in front the bus and poked my head out to see what was coming and that's when they hit me.'

I thought, it could have happened like that, or, she could have been in such a hurry to get back and make me jealous with lies about a date, she weren't looking properly. She had started lying about seeing guys, but I didn't believe her or care before now. But now I cared! After a few weeks, Jasmine's face was cool and she was well on her way to making a full recovery and we was looking to take the boy dem for whatever we could get.

They had been speeding without their lights and they didn't think to slow down when they see a bus parked at a bus stop. I understand she should have looked better, but they were driving erratically regardless, these public servants needed to know what they supposed to be doing out here. Protecting and serving! If you think about it, they were too close to the bus so as she came into view it was all too late, the side mirror caught her square on her chin knocking her and her teeth out. The shock kept her awake long enough to tell the boy dem what number I lived at and what my name was, then she passed out and woke up when I got there. As I stood over her, I thought about what we were arguing over and it was long. What if she had stepped out a second earlier? Them pussy holes would have knocked her into the sky and killed my Missus leaving me on bad terms. I didn't want that, so now I was back to being nice and really supportive. And on top of that, the boy dem were trying to say it weren't their fault. Jasmine really loved me now, she couldn't hide it even if she wanted to. The problem was, it made her even more possessive and clingy. I was all she wanted and because of that, she was stifling me even worse than before.

NOT ME

CHAPTER THIRTY-SEVEN

Summer was coming back around and I was a little bored with Westminster. So I was thinking about going Hammersmith. These times, Merv had done alright in his graphics design college, so he was getting ready to go London College of Fashion. Squeaks had got into a lot of shit, so he was trying to roll with me and do the college ting. Castro had left Kingsway and he was working in a photo shop in West End behind Oxford Street. Facety was working at the same spot he started working when he left school, with his dad doing car body repair. Oki was in Totty more time working in one barber shop, so he weren't really around again. Justin was still in jail, I didn't know when I was gonna see him again. All the rest of the old school man dem were on their own ting now, I didn't know what was going on for most of them.

One Saturday we were bored, broke and on it. It was me, Castro, Merv and Ear, we decided to go try get some garms. Merv was on Selfridges. I told man, 'If we going to do this, it don't make sense going Selfridges.'

Selfridges had been rinsed by man all over London, it weren't the same party - a free for all. But Merv didn't want to listen. Me and Ear just chilled out on this one, we were trying to wait and see wha gwan. I thought *fuck it, let me catch some joke.* I didn't even know Castro was gonna try as they went and done their ting. Now we ready to leave, I'm looking at Merv, he looks bait. He's looking around cause the Security are blatantly on us, casually following, I thought *shit, they on him!* We went down one flight of stairs, then another, but I noticed as we got to the ground floor looking for an exit, they weren't on Merv. All now, Merv was close to steady running. Then I started thinking, *who are they on? It's not me or Ear, we never done nothing, Castro, sneaky rass!* Now I see Castro looking bait, he was calm until he noticed they were on him so now he picked up the pace, he left the store running. Big Oxford Street Castro's on his toes leading the way, closely followed by the Security, then us behind the Security. He buss a right, then a left and ended up in a hotel begging the cashier to hide him. He had asthma too, so he was struggling. We see the Security stop by the hotel, so we thought we'd go in and look to see if we could find him. The first place we looked was the toilet, man figured he'd probably be in there trying to get rid of the shit, but he weren't in there. As we came out the toilet, we started walking towards the exit. Two Black men came walking towards us, talking about, 'There they are.'

I looked around like, *they ain't talking about us,* but it was us they were talking about. They came and grabbed us like it's cool to grab man like that. The worm on me sneaked a serious choke hold on my neck and eased me to the floor quickly. We in this upper class hotel and these Black security guards are treating us like scum. This guy holding me was a real prick, he slyly cut off my air supply so I couldn't breathe. I just relaxed and stopped struggling, wondering what this guy's really doing. The one that was less of a prick, he could see this guy was going way too far, so he told him to get off me and he held me instead.

When I got up, I said, 'What the fuck are you doing you little pussy hole? Don't ever in your life touch me again.' Then I turned to the other guy and told him, 'Tell this prick, don't even look at me or I'll knock it out.'

The real prick turned his attention to Ear and twisted Ear's arm, had man steady screaming all the way down the stairs. When we got to the bottom of the stairs, they found out it weren't us and Castro was in handcuffs. In all the hype, I didn't realise this guy had buss (cut) my lip. I was extra pissed, after I was actually innocent. We walked back to Selfridges with Castro and these Security pussy holes holding him in cuffs.

When we got back, I said, 'I should press charges,' but I didn't know nothing about pressing charges. I didn't have any faith in the system. Why would I, the police were corrupt. I didn't believe he was gonna be punished or even disciplined, so it would have been pointless. By this time, Castro looked like he wished he never done it. His bottom lip was dry and shaking and I could see he was looking company.

I told Castro, 'We link back on the endz cuz!'

But all the way home I was pissed, this little Security pussy hole mugged me off. I was interested to hear what Merv had to say though, he had done well. I dialled him in when I got back on the endz. He was giggling, asking, 'What happened?' talking about, 'I got home cool and I'm shotting (selling) the bits.'

We laughed at what happened to Castro and I told him about the pussy hole ramping with me and Ear. Castro got back on the endz later that night. He said,'They told me never to come back in my life.'

Man had been through enough for the day, so I didn't take the piss out of his dry lip and remind him how it was shaking.

That weekend I made up my mind I was going Hammersmith and West London College. I'd been thinking about it for a while, but Jasmine's people were there and I didn't really want her people eyeballing me but I thought *fuck it, I'm going anyway.* When I told Jasmine she was feeling real (happy). She felt like Rebecca would keep a good eye on me and she would have another reason she could just show up and check on me. I wanted to go there because it was the other live college off the endz. A lot of my people had already gone there and I knew that on the way to and from college, something or someone would always keep me occupied. I was still enjoying the fact I could do whatever I liked and no one cared.

A LITTLE BAIT

CHAPTER THIRTY-EIGHT

When I started Hammersmith, Squeaks enrolled with me same time. It was about an hour journey so we had to leave about eight am to get there on time. We would always see June Sarpong leaving for work before she turned big and forgot about us little guys on the endz. She used to talk non-stop for her whole journey to King's Cross. We didn't get a chance to speak most times, but June was cool and I remembered thinking, she would be good on TV, she don't stop talking. That year when we got to Hammersmith, a few of the man dem from Westminster decided to change and go Hammersmith too - Hard Back and Andy! But I enrolled on I.T and they stayed with P.E so we had different breaks. We were still cool, but now Hard Back was on his endz, he rolled with his West bredrin, Giant. Andy would still link man and chill, but it weren't often. In my class it was me, Squeaks, Dre and Blacker. Blacker shot the weed. He was the first man I knew who sold five-pound draws. That's the only reason he was there and he must of made likkle P's still. Little Dre was man dem, he was from Ladbroke Grove and everyone knew and had love for little Dre. More time it was me, Squeaks and Dre rolling. Common room, breaks, going Hammersmith train station on those after college moves - It was us. Jups and the old man dem left that year I came. I was feeling that college though. It was hype. The way Hammersmith was, as you came in you would have to walk up through a little pathway, then into the square where everyone in the common room would see you. If you were trying to hide, you couldn't. I remember sitting down in the common room chilling and watching bare madness, it might have been Asians and Somalians, it might have been one on one or group fights, but it came like the arena. Sometimes the whole square was full of guys fighting. Back then, borers and gas had been cracked down on a little, so in gang fights, man had started using their belts. Everyone had them metal belts at the time, I never got lashed with one, but you could just tell it would hurt. Trust me, some of those scuffs were nuts. Belts and bottles flying, blood all over the place.

The first day Jasmine came to the college, she came with Rebecca. I knew who Rebecca was but I didn't care about her, like she didn't care about me. They rolled with another chick named Flower. She was Rebecca's right hand chick in the college and I didn't care for either of them. Jasmine introduced us and left it at that. I went about my business. I felt like a big man. *Big man don't have to worry about chicks and what they doing. Chicks have to worry what we doing.* I knew Jasmine was hoping Rebecca kept a good eye on me though.

I'll admit, in Hammersmith, Rebecca did have me feeling a little bait. I knew she was waiting for me to do something she could run back to Jasmine and talk about and she was always around, like she didn't have class. So I didn't enjoy my time there as much as I should have. I found myself having to sneak around to find chicks in places like the library. And there weren't that many I wanted to beat chilling there. I only beat a few chicks in there without Jasmine finding out.

Karren was the most exciting one night stand I managed in Hammersmith. Bigger had beat it already, but I didn't care. She was alright. She was a few years older than me, but I could work with her. When I drawed her and we talking, she asked me where I was from.

I told her,'Walthamstow.'

She said,'I know someone from there,' and asked me if I knew Bigger.

I weren't sure if I should tell her, he's my bredrin and we roll, but I did and it was cool. I convinced her to come chill with me that evening cause, by now, I was a cocky and I could see she was attracted to my confidence. That night she came home with me and we beat in peace surprisingly but I just weren't 100% happy with my performance. She was cool with it, but I knew I could have done a lot better. When I was good, I was good, but there was some pumpum that was having me a little weak, like this one. *We always learning!*

OH SHIT

CHAPTER THIRTY-NINE

Christmas 1996, I remember tings getting a little sticky for me cause Jasmine was maturing nicely, so new bad man was showing her love. It was around the time Castro's cousin was having her birthday party in Chimes. We had been planning to go for ages. Jasmine was going too with her Lady Force girls. They were gonna meet us there.

On the Thursday before the dance, I picked up some crazy virus. I was hot sweating, then cold shivering, throwing up from my mouth and dribbling out me batty. I was weak! But I had talked the talk so I was going. Jasmine was shook though, she knew this one guy that was on her was going and he was on this ting. I knew she didn't want him to see us together. Chimes was a trouble spot too, everyone knew it.

Some might have thought I was asking for trouble. It was a little bit nuts though, Karlene having her party in Hackney, when she was from Tottenham. Tension was still high with Hackney and Tottenham over Popcorn. That was always gonna be a problem. Girls always invited man to a dance too. All them egos in one dance meant trouble. What I did know was, with Jasmine there, it was gonna be an interesting night. I spoke to her on the Saturday and she said, 'We still going?'

So I said, 'I'll see you there.'

From I touched down this dance was jam. Bare man inside though, but I weren't watching that. I was expecting to see Jasmine at anytime. It was a weird night. You could cut the tension in there with a knife. A mad ting! Castro had a fight with some brea trying to draw his Missus. A few other fights kicked off randomly in the midst of gunshots popping off every minute. But gun shot in Chimes was normal, bad man stayed in the dance. The DJ's were nice though, mixing down big tunes. I remember walking back to man dem after having another look for Jasmine and seeing two guys leaving by the fire exit in a hurry. I noticed, but I didn't pay it too much attention. That's until I see this guy dead on the floor, blood running from his head. I thought, OH SHIT! The doors got locked down and no one was allowed to leave. We all got forced into the smallest room like cattle. It took long for them to start letting people out because the boy dem set up video cameras and shit so they could watch us as we left. One at a time they allowed us out for questioning. The camera was looking directly at us, while the police asked questions and took our details. While all this was going on, I was right at the back. It was too hot and at this point, I'm feeling like I should have stayed home. I see bare man going toilet to drop their weapons. They were shook with all this boy dem attention.

Then this guy walks towards the toilet, he weren't scared like the rest so I wondered wha gwan for him. As I watched him, I realised it was heat that had him. As he walked towards the door, he did a skip and a hop, then he twisted and fell in a tidy heap right beside me with his back leaning against the wall, like he meant to take a seat. I shouldn't have laughed, but it's the way he did it. I didn't know him either so I didn't help. (SMH)

Karma had shit ready for me though. It weren't just him the heat was having up, it had me too. I needed to get out, I was boiling up in there. I thought, *let me try hurry the ting up* by making my way to the exit. As I started walking, I felt this feeling come over me. I'd never felt like this before. Castro and Merv 's sister was nearest to me, I just remember holding her arm and telling her, 'Hold me up! Please, hold me up! I don't know what's wrong, just hold me up!'

She said, 'Ah, Chris, you're hurting my arm!'

Then Martin, her baby daddy grabbed me. That's all I remembered before waking up on the other side of the room, next to the bar thinking, *what the fuck just happened?* Guys all around looking at me funny. I knew something had gone really wrong. My knee was killing me too. I got in the car after the boy dem questioned me and took my details and just waited. It was freezing and I just wanted to go home.

WASTING TIME

CHAPTER FORTY

The love I had for Jasmine after her accident had gone all now, as the months had passed cause she had gone back to her normal self. She was even more possessive than before. She was starting to really stress me, taking possessiveness to a new level. She didn't like me moving with certain man because she couldn't handle them, so she was out here trying to cut me off from everyone. She knew they were telling me how to handle her and she didn't want that. She used to hate me chilling at Facety's yard. His yard was the spot us man chilled at more time, tru his mum was blessed and she was the best cook on the endz. When Jasmine realized that cutting me off from the man dem couldn't work, she came up with another more effective plan. She aligned herself with Facety's chicks.

Leanne was Facety's main chick, but he liked to fuck around, like we all did. Maria was the new main fuck-around so her and Jasmine became friends tru they were always around each other cause of us. It was a good way to keep an eye on me, being close with everyone around me. I have to admit, she was good at what she done. I had trouble shaking her and I could see it was gonna get worse.

I left Hammersmith about eight months after I started. I could see I was just wasting time cause I weren't going class. From school, everyone had chosen a different path. Some went straight to work, some went to college and some became career criminals. I didn't realise at the time that the choices I was making were going to limit my options. I felt like I was middle of the road, I weren't totally a criminal, but I was an opportunist. I was maintaining, I was one of the top barbers on the endz and it had its advantages. I was trimming bare man and even though it didn't make crazy P's - when you make a man look fresh, man and man had a certain love for you. So you would get brought in on certain money-making moves.

At the time, one of me close bredrins was working in a popular West End clothes shop. He knew some guys stealing garms there. These guys stole expensive garms and sold them to us for next to nothing. Tru my bredrin worked there, he came up with a tidy little scam. What we done was, take the items back to exchange putting a little extra money on top, to get the cash receipt. Then, we would take whatever it was back and get the full cash refund. I was in charge of taking the garms back and getting the money. It was very tidy and after a while we needed help, so I brought a couple guys in. It run until the shop realised how much money they were losing. Us man changed their policy on returning goods.

ALWAYS CAUSING
A PROBLEM

CHAPTER FORTY-ONE

All now Merv had the college ting locked the best. London College of Fashion was moving. The bar was nice, bare girls went there and Merv was the man up in there. In his class there was Corina, Charlotte and Selina. I was feeling Corina tru her face and body was smooth. By now, I weren't letting little things like fucked-up hair do's and shoes dictate what a pretty chick was. She was sexy. Charlotte was sexy too, but really short, too short for me. Selina was alright in the face, she had a decent size for me too, but she didn't really wow me. There was something about her, a little bit weird. She seemed focused on her ting. She always said, 'I know what you lot are like, I don't want that for myself!' I accepted what she said and I left her alone. Merv fucked Corina and Squeaks fucked Charlotte. I didn't fuck no one! *It's a good thing I left Selina alone.(I'll tell you later)*

After I left Hammersmith, I thought I'd get my head down and do some work. I knew I was wasting time and even though I didn't have a plan, I thought I'd better do something. Some of the man dem were getting ready to go Uni. What the fuck was I doing? I felt the pressure to fix up.

I choose Islington ITEC. It was a quiet college and just

what I needed, nothing like my normal. It was offering NVQs and that would be enough for me go straight to Uni. There weren't no chicks in this one, just a few man, one Hackney man who I used to travel back to the endz with. And one man from Kings Cross, a few years older than us and that's why Jasmine loved it. She didn't have to worry about nothing. She slept peaceful at night, me going there. I knew I was there to study, but the study ting was long. I weren't really on it, so I was surprised when I ended up just making the grade. The teachers weren't on their ting. They didn't notice I hadn't done all the work, so they helped and passed me. To be honest, I'm surprised I could concentrate on anything other than Jasmine at the time, she had me nervous. She had moved into the house next door to Lady Force Vanessa and she wanted me there every night. If for some reason I weren't there or she didn't know exactly where I was, it was peak (trouble). She wanted to speak to me before I went to bed and as soon as I woke up every morning. If I didn't answer her call in the morning for whatever reason, no one would get through to me until I answered her call. It could have been for the whole day. She wouldn't stop ringing. Sometimes I left my phone at home on purpose, just to have a break from her and I'd come back to 80 or 90 missed calls. She was causing my *cool* all kind of problems. Mumsy was even getting pissed off with her. Jasmine loved me so much, now it was scary. She was making scenes on road anywhere. If we were on road and we saw a chick she knew I would be feeling, she'd go nuts - like I'd drawed the chick already.

Screaming, 'WHAT, YOU WANT TO FUCK THAT BITCH CHRIS?'

I should have whacked her up for how she was having me. But I was trying to be nice and now I was starting to lose stripes. Man was talking to me like, *Fuck me Sibs, what's wrong with you? You can't manage this chick, don't let her have you up like this.* I was feeling weak out here. Smoking weed daily to chill me the fuck out, cause every day had the potential to be another madness. She was earning stripes off me and it was nuts. She was the first chick on the planet that was having me up, I needed to snap out of it. She was at my house a few days a week, acting like it's her house. The bitch was threatening to tell the boy dem about the tings I had around me and scams us man were popping. She was really taking the piss, with new muscles, the muscles she was getting from me. She went deep with her fuckery, she even managed to get my Mum's work number and started calling her at her work place. This chick was nuts, phoning Mumsy's house phone all times of night, being disrespectful and showing man no ratings. It was all too much!

Man weren't dissing me in my face, but I know behind my back, it was big talk on the endz. Castro was telling me what he'd be doing all now, if it was him. I was saying to myself, *'You're a G!'* Facety was giving me real advice too, but I didn't want it to seem like I was doing exactly what man said. I felt like I should have known how to deal with this madness myself, even though I'd never been in the situation before. I was beating myself up about it. I'm not encouraging beating women, but my first mistake was telling her I would never beat her. And my second mistake was, not beating her. It seemed like that's all she respected. I was suffering from 'too-sweet-boy syndrome.'

I'M NOT ADDICTED

CHAPTER FORTY-TWO

One evening, out in Leyton talking about the *bitch* to the man dem, crack came into my life. I'd been smoking weed a little while now, even though I'd never smoked cigarette. I knew that weed improved the taste, but crack, it made smoking taste nice. It was like smoking sweets. I had seen crack fuck with man for years on the endz and now I could see why, but crack weren't gonna fuck with me, I thought. A few of my man dem was on it, but they seemed to have it under control.

That evening when I tried it, the taste sweet me and it filled my mind with bad thoughts. Man called it the 'bad boy' for a real reason. I see straight away, how it could get man. The side effect for me was a bad attitude and that night I went home and took that bad attitude with me. Jasmine saw something was different straight away and she didn't like it. She didn't know what it was at first, but I was different. That night I changed and it changed our relationship for good. I had had enough of her shit and I was going to make her pay. She used to like us fighting, cause after, we'd make up and I'd give her good body. But now, after everything she'd put me through, I'd had enough. Over the next few weeks, I started showing her, if you ain't gonna let me go, I'm gonna make you live with things you really don't want to live with. The change in me was so drastic - so quick, I think I reminded her of her uncle.

She asked me one evening, 'Chris, have you been smoking crack?'

I told her straight, 'Yeah, I've been smoking crack and I like it!'

She was shocked that I was so blatant about it, but by now, I didn't give a shit what she thought.

I told her same time, 'Listen, I'm fucking other chicks, why don't you just fuck off and leave me alone.'

Jasmine was losing the bass in her voice, but she was a fighter, she weren't going down without a fight.

Around the time, I had some computer books I was into, sometimes more than her and them books cost me P's. After one crazy argument, I went out to cool off and come back, to see the bitch had ripped them all up, smashed all my aftershave and on top of that she's chilling laughing, like, *what the fuck are you gonna do?* It was rage! I had to toe punt her for that. She called the boy dem to Mumsy's house, telling them I had a gun. It was only my new one pop, but the police came. When they got to the yard and they saw what she was going on with they left me with my one pop and she left my yard that night for good. She still wouldn't let me go though, but now she couldn't come to Mumsy's.

She latched on even harder to Facety's chicks. Petra was the new one, der in Hackney. We used to go there some times to sit down and chill. That's where Jasmine caught me one night testing food (smoking crack). She looked scared! And something in her eye I saw that night made me stop. She had seen how it had changed her uncle and I had seen how it had fucked up the endz. I knew I couldn't let it get me, like it had got so many man. But the stinking attitude stayed. I wasn't addicted to nicotine and that's what saved me, but for a little while, I was smoking shit and getting fucked up on it too. I weren't a waste man by nature so that life was never me and I had things to do.

ME, UNI, WOW!

CHAPTER FORTY-THREE

I was trying to get into the computer ting. I could see it was the future. I had bought some books on Dos, the Window's operating system, tru the Government was talking about all computers are going to crash in the year 2000. I was trying to learn some real shit! I was going Uni now! Who would have thought after everything that had happened in my life so far, *I'd* be going Uni, I couldn't believe it. I had options - *Me* with Uni options. I was thinking, either Westminster, South Bank or Luton. I went to the South Bank open day and as Jasmine was holding on to this relationship by the skin of her teeth, I let her know. *It's only tru I had a plan.* It was college time for her all now and I knew, if I made her think I was going South Bank, tru she was nuts and I knew it well, she would decide she wants to go South Bank College and that's exactly what she done. When she told me she'd enrolled at South Bank College I was chuffed; she didn't know I had changed and enrolled at Luton. In my mind it was a done deal. The time we'd spend together would only be when I came back to London some weekends.

Jasmine had different ideas though. This chick was mad.

I'm out here trying to get rid of the bitch and she's here pushing herself on me even more.

Winston was the older from Kings Cross. I had met at The ITEC College. He had told me he had some bredrins up in Luton renting rooms. I told him I needed one cause I was going up there, so he introduced us. The guy's name was Richard and this property he had to rent weren't nice, but it was cheap and I needed somewhere quick. I was starting the following week. It was in a decent location but more than that I was desperate, so I moved in there on the Sunday, Two days after my 19th birthday 1997, before classes started on the Tuesday. And cause I was the last one, I ended up with the smallest room.

I told Jasmine on my birthday, 'Look, I'm going to live in Luton! You know I like to fuck and I'm going to fuck. I'll still fuck you if you like, but nothing sweets a man like me more than new pumpum.'

It had been her way for years. I'd had enough. It had to stop.

She said, 'I understand what you're saying babes, but you don't need to fuck anyone else if I'm there for you.'

She decided to make it her mission to be around when ever I wanted to fuck. And I made it *my* mission to want to fuck more than she was around. It was the highest disrespect. I was dissing her all now and she was just having it.

She even helped me unpack after I told her, 'I'm gonna be fuck-fuck-fucking!' and she stayed with me that first night.

That evening after I packed away my shit, I went for a walk, me one, to see wha gwan for Luton. I was strolling by the Arndale Centre when I see Samoda. He was one of the older Totty man. We talked about the endz, man and man and the madness that was going on, then what's good for Luton. He told me he's starting on Tuesday, like me. I smiled and thought, *Luton ain't going to be so bad still.*

As I travelled back to the yard, Merv holla'd to see where

I was and wha gwan for the endz. He was like my shadow all now, but I didn't mind him around me most of the time. Things with his dad had got that bad, his dad didn't care if he came home at night or not. I knew he'd be chilling with me for days at a time when I got settled. He did let me settle in, I aint gonna lie, but it only took a few days before he was part of the furniture. He would come, no toothbrush, no cash, no nothing not even money for food, forget the train ticket. It was normal to bump the train and duck the inspectors, but it didn't take long before I started wondering if Merv was going to start costing me money too.

Back on the endz, after a few weeks settling into Luton life, I saw Donnie on a random one. I told him I was in Luton studying.

He told me, 'I've got a bredrin called Marshal studying law in Luton too, you should link him, he's big up there, you'll find him if you look.'

I took Donnie's number cause I hadn't seen him for a while, I wanted to talk to him about his music ting too. When I went back up, I looked for Marshal and found him during that week. It was always good to have a strong link already set on the endz. Marshal made things nice for me in them early days. He showed me what was good and who to link and for what. When I enrolled in Luton, I wanted to do Computer Science, but all the places were full so an advisor told me, 'Enrol on something else, then, change when guys drop out.'

I took his advice and enrolled on Computer Aided Design.

This class was full of guys that had studied CAD in college. They knew CAD well. I wasn't ready for CAD, so as soon as I got a chance to move, I did. Computer Science was more like it for me, but it was a big class and by now I was rolling with the man dem that got to class late, sat round the back where we couldn't hear shit and pretty much fucked around, the same as I had done in college.

WHAT AM I DOING

CHAPTER FORTY-FOUR

During the days I was at Uni, I left Merv in the house. He would hit road early afternoon to see if any money could make or he could draw any chicks. I would holla him when I was leaving to see where he was and if he had found anything good for us to work on or work with for the evening.

The sad reality was, I went to Uni to waste a few more years, but be able to say I was doing something constructive. *Fucked up I know, I wasn't ready for Uni!* I knew all Mumsy wanted, was to say I'm in Uni; so I figured I'd do that for a while till something real came up. Within a few weeks, I knew everyone who was going on with tings in Uni and I was getting to know the guys going on with tings that didn't go Uni, but lived in Berry Park where I lived. Berry Park was full of Asians making a lot of money from brown (heroin). Them man dealt large amounts of drugs because of the airport, so they kind of controlled Luton. The guys who owned my house knew who was who in Berry Park, so they made sure they knew who I was.

Jasmine had started in South Bank all now. I didn't think she was serious when she said she would come up and be with me while I was in Luton, but she was. She really was. She packed her clothes in the morning, left for college from mine in Luton, then jumped on a train straight from there back to Luton every day, on a real long ting. Then on the weekends, we'd leave and go to London together.

One weekend back on the endz I saw Marky, Bones and Dred walking, as me and Jasmine walked towards the park, we stopped to talk. Bones and Dred, were foundation older's that were always around back in the day, Marky's man dem. It had been a hot minute (long time) since I'd seen them man. I told them where I was and that's when Bones told me he was enrolling in Luton in February. It was big to hear an older was gonna show face in the same Uni as me and they hadn't seen how I was big all now. When I got back to Luton, I started telling man, one of my olders from my endz is coming to study with us, he's studying Computer Science too.

Marky and them had to rate me all now, I could see they was. I remember them looking at Jasmine. I knew what they were thinking, if I weren't there and they saw her randomly walking they would have been on her quickly. We exchanged numbers and we started linking again. Bones told me he was going to start making plans to move up in January. By now, I had linked some nice Uni chicks and man was earning stripes as one of the name brand guys in my year. Not only that, I was telling Jasmine in detail all the shit I was doing. Shit had changed. She hated how I had her now, but I didn't care. I was going to break her, the same way she had tried to break me if she stayed.

One sexy dark-skin chick from Birmingham was my first victim. Sabrina her name was. She had all the things I like, just how I liked them. I drawed her doing likkle food shopping in the Arndale Centre one afternoon. That same night, Chin, James and Richard were going London. Chin and James were my room mates, so I was going to be the only one in the house for the night. I was cool with that; Jasmine wasn't around this evening and neither was Merv so I thought, *yeah I'll find something to do.* It was about 8 and Richard and the rest had left about 20 minutes now. I needed the chicken shop tru I didn't feel like cooking, so I left out, but forgot my key like a dickhead. No one was going to be back for the rest of the night so I was fucked. Then I thought, *I should holla Sabrina.* She's only 10 minutes down the road. I knew it was a bit cheeky, tru I had just drawed her that day, but I *was* a bit cheeky.

I phoned her and explained, 'Them man have left for London, I've locked myself out like an idiot, they're not gonna be back till morning. I've got nowhere to sleep. Can you help me?'

She said, 'Yeah, no problem, come round.'

I said to myself, *ah, she's letting me come over, she's bless!* So I made my way to her house and she opened the door looking sexy and shit. She had one friend I didn't like cause she was too much like a man, but she was upstairs. I snuck in cause I knew it didn't look good and I was thankful for the favour. I told her as well, as we stayed up watching a movie. She lived in a shared house like mine; it was a ting where she had a room with a single bed and everything else was communal.

It was late all now and we both had Uni in the morning, so it was time to sleep. As we lay down on her single bed, obviously, I started kissing her neck while I played with her nipples. They were hard and her breathing was just how I liked it, so when she said, 'You know we can't do this!'

I had to wonder why. As I'm smothering her, making her hot, whispering sweet shit in her ear, I could see I was making her uncomfortable, till she gave up and let me in. By that time she was soaking. I pushed it in deep and felt myself ready to buss straight away. It was sweet, I had to come out and slow it down. I poked her on the outside for a bit then pushed it back deep inside, I felt myself ready to buss again. This one was naughty. I had to take it out for a bit. Then she told me I had to stop. She had a boyfriend back in Birmingham she was still with. I was pissed but I said cool and lowed it.

That morning she woke me up bright and early, telling me it's time for me to go.

I said, 'Thanks for letting me stay,' then tried to kiss her, she gave me her cheek then hurried me to leave. I left, but I had to acknowledge I did like her. That was a pumpum I could get used to, but I knew the game.

When I got back to the house, man had just come back. They asked me, 'Where did you sleep last night blood?'

I told them the story and man couldn't believe it. I hadn't been in the Uni two weeks and already I had chicks letting me stay in their bed.

Jasmine didn't know about that one yet, but I was in a hurry to tell her. Susannah was the next one I met in them first few weeks that stood out a little. She was from Stratford, East London like me. Big tits, light-skin and decent, but she was one of them loud chicks, who loved to be up in the club making noise.

Some evenings, when Jasmine weren't around, I'd chill at her place where her and her friends stayed, another shared house about 15 minutes from mine in the opposite direction from Sabrina. She was feeling me hard and I did like fucking her, even though she didn't sweet me like Sabrina did.

In hindsight, I should have told her about Jasmine tru Jasmine was crazy and she did have a right to know. But the truth was, I didn't tell her because in all honesty I wanted Jasmine out of my life, so why would I tell anyone about her? I wanted to forget about her.

GUESS WHAT

CHAPTER FORTY-FIVE

One Sunday evening it all came out though. I was about 6 weeks into Luton life. My roommate James fucked me up and he knew what he was doing. He didn't like me and Merv doing it so big already, after he weren't getting shit. He was feeling Jasmine too and he probably felt like she was too good for me or he would treat her better. He was stupid as well as a hater. Chin was cool, he weren't a gyalis (girl's man) like me, but he done his ting. He had pumpum and he wouldn't hate on a man, but James... James knew on Sundays I came back to Luton with Jasmine all the time. There was never a Sunday so far when Jasmine wasn't with me. I was fucking Susannah, not him and me and Susannah hadn't made no arrangements this evening.

I'd just finished giving Jasmine cock, so I had my towel on watching TV. I was getting ready to put it on her again, when we heard the door open. I didn't think nothing of it, I thought *it must be James or Chin getting back from London.*

Jasmine said, 'Oh someone's here, let me go and ask one of them for a cigarette.'

I didn't have a problem with that, until Jasmine run back upstairs all excited saying, 'Guess who's downstairs with

James?'

I said, 'Who?'

I didn't like the excitement in her voice.

She said, 'Susannah!' as she ran off back downstairs.

I had told Jasmine I was fucking, I had even given names, so I knew it was on. I took a few seconds to wonder what the fuck James had done, then I composed myself, put some clothes on and went downstairs.

I said, 'Wha gwan Susannah, you cool?'

By now, Jasmine's up in her face calling her a bitch and a whore. Telling her, 'You've been fucking my man.'

I said,'Cool the fuck out, Jasmine, what you going on with!'

She said, 'Tell this bitch I'm your girl and she's just a fuck.'

I didn't want to do that really because I liked fucking Susannah, little things she done turned me on. And I didn't give a shit about Jasmine, she just wouldn't let me go.

James was there with his weasel face saying, 'I didn't mean to cause a problem.'

I said, 'James, you knew Jasmine would be here, why bring Susannah?'

He talked some shit about, 'I wasn't thinking, I'm really sorry.'

But I could see this situation was going to make or break me on the endz, so I played it cool.

I said,'You know what, I'm gonna leave you guys here to talk, I'm gonna go fuck Sabrina.'

I put on my jacket then left the yard. I wasn't going to fuck Sabrina. I hadn't fucked Sabrina since that first time. As I came out the house, I thought to myself, *what the fuck am I really gonna do now? This is sticky. I've left these chicks in my house and I'm talking about going to fuck some other chick, I'm not even really gonna fuck.*

I phoned Marshal, I needed to talk to someone sensible. I

broke the situation down to him. I was going to walk down to his, but I thought about it and said 'No,' I need to go back to my yard and deal with this situation, before they come up with some funny plan to try fuck me. About 15 minutes later I came back, let myself in and said, 'So what's the deal, I'm caught! What you want to do about this all now?'

Susannah said, 'How could you do this to me, Chris? You didn't tell me you had a girl! If I knew, I wouldn't of let things go where they did!'

I said, 'You're right, I should have told you I had a girl, but I didn't!'

Then Jasmine said, 'Tell her, Chris, tell her I'm wifey and she's just a fuck!'

I said, 'Yeah, she's right, she's wifey,'*even though she weren't*, 'and you're just a fuck!'

Then that situation was over. Susannah went home feeling used and I went back to bed and gave Jasmine more cock. Nothing more was said on the matter. Susannah was with her friend and it didn't look good. James really tried to fuck me and have witnesses, but I came out like a G. I was slowly taking back control of my life and it felt good. I looked like the man, James looked like a hater, Susannah looked like a home-wrecking whore, but I felt bad for her still and made it known I was sorry, I really was, I knew about Karma.

BREAKING AWAY SLOWLY

CHAPTER FORTY-SIX

Bones was der in Luton all now, looking somewhere to live. I let him stay at mine a few nights until he found somewhere, tru he's one of my foundation olders. The first spot he found was near town, on top of our regular chicken shop we backed after Uni. It was dingy bad. I wouldn't have stayed there, not even a night. Bones must have stayed there one night and never went back. The location was the only thing live about that spot, trust me; just by the Arndale Centre.

Richard and his bredrin Martin rented flats round there, but their flats were nice, expensive as well. When you looked at them man, you could see they were making money. I wanted in on their hustle, houses and flats to rent, always driving nice whips. It come like they had whole heap of disposable income. So, it weren't long before (when I was supposed to be in class learning my books) I was travelling England and Wales with them man looking new opportunity off the endz and making Jasmine jealous same time.

She hated when I took those trips. It would have been worse if she knew them man were womanisers; and they found wealthy old women to fuck, then swindle. If I could have brought myself to do that shit, I would have been in a hurry to tell her. I just couldn't! Even though it was working for them.

Some of them trips were a madness though; I didn't know people off the endz were keeping up with some of what I saw. Crackheads and poverty was serious everywhere we went. And it's tru them country man could smell a London man a mile off, someone always assumed we were the new local drug dealers. I met hit men in Gloucester looking work; and prostitutes in Bristol, begging us to bring them back to the endz to work.

We actually brought one of them back. Martin saw some potential in her, I didn't know what he was looking at though cause I couldn't see it. She was dead (ugly)! Ok, she weren't totally dead in the face, but man knew I was a gyalis. If I'm telling man I'm pimping, they gonna assume it's a certain level and this chick weren't on the level. *I guess I just had a problem selling things I wouldn't buy.* I didn't feel comfortable telling the Uni man I've got this chick working - looking like she did. But when I think about it, guys like my roommate who weren't getting nothing would have been on it; so it should have been a money spinner still. I just didn't see it like that at the time.

I ended up looking after her sometimes in the house when clients came round. She always asked me why I didn't fuck her like everyone else did or why I never told her to suck it. I could see in her eyes she would have swallowed all my babies, but she weren't getting them, not even in her mouth. She stayed making money for us for a while though; but she started missing her family, so we let her go back to her endz.

Them man was pissed cause it was easy money, so we were all on the lookout for a new chick for a while. I didn't look for long though cause I knew it was wrong. I wouldn't have liked one of my family members to be pimped, so in the end I forgot about pimping.

These times, Bones was still having trouble finding a spot he was happy with, so he would still stay at mine certain time. Now he'd been on the endz a while, as time went on I noticed, bringing him in on tings could be a bit of a boo-boo. He weren't that smooth. On the endz back in the day, man had ratings for Bones cause he was an older. But now he's here, he's talking a lot of shit, embarrassing man and blaming it on the weed. I had promoted him as a big man and Merv was looking bigger, making more moves and getting a lot more pussy.

FUCKING WITH MY SHIT

CHAPTER FORTY-SEVEN

By now, Jasmine was easily the biggest problem in my life. I just didn't want to hear from her, see her or anything. If I left my phone to ring, she would message me telling me she's going to ring my phone till I either pick up or my battery dies. People around me would notice I was stressing, she had me thinking about her every minute and I didn't know what to do with this chick. She was mad, to where I didn't know women acted like that. I had never seen anything like it. That Easter of '98 I told Jasmine I wouldn't be seeing her anymore. I'd just had enough!

I had two cars all now; a sports car and a comfortable car. I decided to drive the comfortable whip back to the endz tru it was the smoother drive and the drive was a lot of motorway.

When I told her, she said,'I want to come talk to you about it.'

I said, 'Jasmine, its long, there's no point. We over! I don't ever want to see you again. I'm going London for Easter anyway, so coming to see me in Luton's long.'

She knew she weren't allowed in Mumsy's house again, she had blown up my Mum's house phone to the point where my Mum had to change it. That pissed Mumsy right off, she'd had that number since we moved there and now cause of this bitch, she was having to change it. Not only that, Mumsy had been good to her over the years, so to be disrespecting her like that was alot. I thought about it after I told her I was going to London, I knew I shouldn't have told her that. She was going nuts on the phone, I remember her bawling out of control.

Even though I didn't care about her tears, I knew she was going to do something. She was slowly getting the message though, but who was I going to have while she was still deh keeping up with madness? She had tried hard to cut me off from everyone on the endz and to an extent it had worked. Giving her a slap all now was nothing, I didn't mind seeing her cause she could get that. But she weren't leaving me just like that, I knew it, so I had to expect something. And I was!

I got down to London wondering what she's gonna do next. A few hours had passed and I hadn't heard anything, but hearing nothing from her in this situation weren't a good thing. All the time I weren't hearing from the bitch, I knew she was doing something. I just didn't know what, until she called me from my house in Luton.

'I've just fuck up your car, Chris, you should see it,' she said.

I could hear the happiness in her voice.

'What the fuck did you do you bitch?' I said.

She liked to fuck with shit that didn't belong to her. She had smashed the windows and bored up the tyres. I remember thinking, *am I going to have to kill this bitch to get her out my life?*

MORE DRAMA!

CHAPTER FORTY-EIGHT

Jasmine was fucking up everything and I really couldn't see a way out. I asked Vanessa, my friend studying in Luton, to talk to her. I knew her from Trocadero days, her and her sister. I was feeling Vanessa, but she knew I was with Jasmine and she knew Jasmine was nuts, so we fell into the friend zone quickly. I introduced them one day and from then they were best friends, always rolling, linking in London and shit. When Mumsy changed her house number, I gave the number to V cause we were tight. I thought I could trust her; but things changed with us because after about a week I started getting them calls (like back in the day) on Mumsy's new house phone, with breathing and silence. I asked V, 'did you give Jasmine the number?'

She said, 'No,' but she was lying. There was no one else she could have got it from. Jasmine was taking the piss, popping off Mumsy's new house phone like nothing's changed. She wouldn't stop phoning.

In the end Mumsy told me she can't take it anymore, tru it was nuts. I felt like a cunt causing Mumsy all this trouble, so I told Mumsy, 'Look, I'll leave and I won't come back till I've sorted this out'.

Mumsy told me, 'Yes, GO!'

So now I'm having to make Luton home. And this bitch is just turning up in Luton cause Vanessa telling her where I might be. I'd see her in clubs looking sexy and shit, but, I knew I had to leave her alone. Bare man was on her too, she was sexy. I really didn't care though who was on her. I was begging someone would take her off my hands. I was encouraging it - her looking for a different life, cause I was.

Donnie was looking for me all now. Marshal told me he'd been trying to get me, but the number he had for me was off. Man didn't know all the problems I was having and how I had changed my number bare times trying to shake the bitch. I had time for Donnie though, so I got the number from Marshal and holla'd him. We talked about family and his group. The group hadn't made it big like he had hoped, but he had kept some links and now he was trying a different ting. He heard I was going on with tings, so he wanted me on board for the new project he was working on. He asked me to keep an eye out for something worth him coming down for, so I holla'd him for one dance I knew was gonna be alright.

I remember queuing, wondering if it was gonna be one of those nights when the bitch showed up; but she didn't and we skanked till morning, then he came back to mine. He saw Luton had love for me, so he wanted me on the team. I told him, 'Holla me when you're ready in it,' tru he was still organising tings back on the endz.

WOW

CHAPTER FORTY-NINE

It was hard for me now I didn't have my base on the endz, going back to London was long. I'd go back on Saturday to trim certain man sometimes, see my dad and see if any extra P could make. Man could get caught up living the country life, tru country was alright and anything could happen.

One weekend I decided to stay in Luton. I phoned T to check he was staying on the endz. He said he was so I told him, 'I'll look for you in your halls either later on or tomorrow.' T and Josh had a little CD business popping, so it kept them busy and someone had to stay in Luton to stay on top of tings. I told him,'I'm bringing some chicks for us to chill with too.'

By now I was the man, so he took me serious. He didn't know I was just talking, I didn't have anything planned. I thought, let me go for a little drive, see what's popping but road was dead. *Nothing ain't going on all now*, so I headed towards T's halls. As I was just round the corner from his yard, I see these two chicks, one ginger and one blonde. I smiled at them and they smiled back, so I pulled up with my confident swag and we started talking. I said,'What's popping, what you girls on for the evening?'

Ginger said, 'Nothing.'

I told her, 'I'm going to link my bredrin and we gonna watch some movies. It's just round the corner in them hall, you girls coming?'

They said,'Yeah,'and jumped in.

I couldn't believe it. So now we der in Milliner's Way, chilling in T's room watching DVDs. We sat in a way where, me and Ginger were at the back and the friend was nearer to T at the front, in the same direction as the TV. We were catching joke still, so after a while of me feeling up Ginger, I told her,'Come.' T had already showed me where the toilets were, so I took her in there and she turned off the light. She told me to sit down, so I sat on the toilet as I felt her up. She was the first white chick I'd ever been with.

This was all new to me and I couldn't really see what was going on, but she got on her knees and started unzipping my trousers. I smiled as she took me out and started rocking the mic - *wow she was good.* She did that ting like a star. I'd never felt it like that before and I think she could tell by my breathing she was having me up. She made my toes curl, then had me buss in her mouth real quick. I couldn't believe she milked me dry and swallowed everything. She even had me feeling bad for not pushing my cock in her belly, how she had me.

When she finished we went back to the bedroom and carried on watching the movie like nothing had happened. I was feeling real though. T couldn't wait to tell me he heard what was going on. I giggled and told him,'She's a fucking star.'

He was pissed cause his one weren't letting off. I would never have expected that afternoon, that, that evening I'd be chilling with a chick that's got a head game anywhere near that. Before her, I'd had girls give me blow jobs, some were ok, some were good, but none were anywhere near this one.

Most made me say, *here look just lay down*, but this chick had taught me a lesson.

It took me about an hour before I was ready to go again. I told her, 'Come,' and we went back to the toilet and she done it all again. As she was doing it this time, I played with her pussy. I had to do something. Her pussy was soaking too, but she didn't even ask me to put it in, so I didn't. She had me cum in under five minutes again. This chick was good; and the fact the sink was right there, but she swallowed all my babies on her knees in front of me, turned me on so much more. She liked to do that and she did it well.

By this time, we'd been in T's since about 11.30pm and now it was coming on 5 in the morning. She had milked me dry and I had no energy left. I was ready for my bed, everyone was, so I told T, 'We leaving, I'll come link you in the hours.' I took her number, then left her to walk. I was a bastard I know. I had her number. I thought, *I'll holla another day soon.* They had to walk far too cause they didn't have no money. I should have dropped her but Jasmine had made me cold. Back in the day, I would have dropped her.

When Bones came back from London on the Sunday, I told him what had happened. He was pissed he weren't around. Now, after what I had told him, he wanted to link Ginger and her friend. I ain't gonna lie, I wanted to link her again too. I thought Ginger was gonna be my local. In my mind I already had plans to sneak off with her when I was bored. She had given me the best head I'd ever had and I hadn't even put it on her yet. I wondered what it would be like, she even had a little back-off.

As I gave him all the little details, I see into his brain as he thought about it. Bones hated my style. I had changed so much since that yute man I was all them years ago and he was having trouble coping.

That week - I tried to link my little star again but I realised she was never home. Bare man must have been keeping her busy with them skills she had. After about a week of trying to holla her daily, I had to let her go cause it was long. Her mum even started recognizing my voice. I couldn't be running down no chicks, it didn't matter how serious she was. After that week, I left her to go down in the history books. *The best head I ever had!!*

GOD WANTS US
TO BE TOGETHER

CHAPTER FIFTY

It had been a while now since I had last seen Mumsy and even though she had upset me, tru I felt like she hadn't supported me, I was missing her. I didn't have anyone I could talk to about personal things, other than the bitch that had caused all the problems I needed to talk about. That made me a little scared to move on, but at the same time I knew I had to. Our relationship was toxic and I could see something bad happening sooner or later, so I was trying to stay away. It had been about two weeks since I'd seen Jasmine. She was slowly getting it.

So imagine, back in London on a weekend, I decided to go Oxford Street to do some shopping. I get on the underground at Walthamstow Central, the first station on the Victoria line. Seven Sisters, the heart of Tottenham, is a few stops away. Who do I see on the platform at Seven Sisters, waiting on a train going Oxford Street? Of all the carriages I could have got on or she could have got on, of all the trains she could have got on. It weren't even like she saw me and had to run up the platform or something. The carriage I was on stopped right there where she was standing.

What the fuck! First, she acted like it was nothing.

I was with Facety and Castro and she said,'Hello,' to them and just chilled out. In her mind, she must have thought, *see, God wants us to be together. How could this happen if it weren't supposed to?* She played cool till it was time to get off the train, that's when she decides she wouldn't let me go.

She held on to me and asked me 'Where do you think you're really going without me?'

She followed me, holding my arm tight for about forty minutes. If I tried to shake her off, she acted like I was beating her, screaming at the top of her voice in big West End. All that excitement was nuts!

To calm her down I told her, 'I'll link you later, I just need time on my own with the man dem right now,' but she thought I was lying. When that didn't work, I got pissed so she tried to make me jealous, she blew a kiss at some brea as he walked past. Tru she was sexy, the brea and his bredrins were looking and on her. As they were walking off they started telling her to come.

I said, 'Look, them breas are calling you, go with them in it!'

The breas could see she was nuts. I was pointing at them; shouting; telling her to fuck off, but she stayed tight on my arm.

Facety ended up telling her, 'Listen, you're pissing me off all now too! Sibs don't want you, you can't see that? FUCK OFF!'

She was with Facety's old bit on the side and even she didn't really want to be there doing all this, so they managed to talk her into leaving, as long as I promised to phone her and link her later in the night.

I realised right there, this chick had actually broken me down. I felt like I wouldn't find a chick that loved me like she does. She done things that weren't normal. That evening I phoned her and we linked at Facety's. I knew I was doing my family wrong linking this chick after everything she'd done. She had caused Mumsy so much stress, my brother so much stress and me so much fucking stress... and now I'm here with her again. *What was I doing?* I was having flashbacks of the evening I toe punted her cause she threatened to throw a brick through Mumsy's front room window, if I didn't come outside and talk to her. I was fucking her because she had made me believe it was easier to just be with her, cause she was crazy and she didn't care who knew. I thought, *if this is how a serious relationship is, I don't ever want another one of these.* Lying there after that, I knew that was it. I had seen the light and I needed to cut her off for good. I stopped taking her calls from then and let her ring off my phone till she got bored for a few weeks, then she tells me in a text: 'Chris, I'm pregnant!'

That hit me hard! The only thing saving me in this ting, was Jasmine wanted a family. Her mum had instilled them values in her, she wanted a husband with her children. So when she told me she was pregnant, I told her straight, 'You can have that yute Jasmine, but you're going to bring it up on your own. We ain't never gonna be a happy family.'

She thought about it and realised I must be serious. She had done so much, she probably thought I would have preferred jail and she was half right.

I told her, 'There's going to be no child support, no nothing, you're going to be a statistic, another black chick with a baby and no baby daddy.'

I was shock to death. If she decided to have that baby she would have got me, but I sold her on the fuckery and tru she had done so much, she thought I was telling the truth. Honestly, I could have never abandoned my baby. I just hoped she had enough doubt.

I had whole heap of plans for the future. I was about to start my music career. I was gonna be a star! That's how I saw it. I didn't want nothing to do with Jasmine, so this yute had to go. I had to convince her and in the end, I did, with all that single-parent talk. She phoned me to tell me she had booked an appointment to have the abortion.

Up in all this madness, Donnie was just finishing up his degree and putting the finishing touches on this record label ting he had been talking about. He let me know, we soon gonna be ready to do business, so it was on. That was a positive in all the negative going on. It gave me some hope for the future.

On the day Jasmine was going to have the abortion, I woke early and rolled out from Luton. I made it down to St Ann's Hospital a little late, so I went to the waiting room. As I came in, she was just being taken into the room.

She kept saying,'Sorry.'

I said, 'You don't have to be sorry.'

In my head I was thinking *you're doing the right thing - just do it*. When they finished the abortion, the nurse said I could go in and talk to her, but I didn't have anything to say when I knew it was done. I gave her a kiss on her cheek and told her,'Take care,' then turned and walked, not looking back. I was cold, that's why I left her like that. She had abused my trust, she had almost broken me and now she was lying there crying, hoping I didn't leave.

Now that weight was off my shoulders, I jumped in the whip and started that long drive back to Luton. I had a lot on my mind! Was she really going to leave me alone? Was I gonna make things right with Mumsy? Was I gonna be that star in this music business? Was I gonna be that victim of Capitalism school taught me to be and get it by any means necessary? It was that time and I wanted mine so *I was soon gonna find out.*

SPECIAL PREVIEW

A PRODUCT OF MY
ENVIRONMENT

PART 2

LIFE IS FUNNY

CHAPTER ONE

A few days later, I saw Joy (shorty from school days that got beat up with her mum in the playground back in the day) strolling in the market. She was always sexy and she was growing nice in her skin, I thought I'd draw her now she's older and try a ting. We started talking so I took her number. I knew exactly who she was but she didn't remember me. She didn't remember I was right there watching her and her mum get a beating. She asked me, 'what school did you go too?'

I told her, 'Holy Family', so she asked, 'do you know Shelly and Aisha?'

I said, 'yes',

Shelly was in my class most of my school life, I couldn't deny her, especially for some pum pum. Then she told me, 'I don't like them girls, but I don't want to talk about it.' That shit was funny but she didn't see me laugh.

I said, 'why, tell me?' all surprised like I didn't know, but she wouldn't. I went and linked her a few days later, at her yard, but she weren't letting off so I lowed it. I told Squeaks - coz I remembered he tried it with her a few years before me. He had acted dumb like he didn't remember either. We laughed as we chilled with Castro at his dad's house.

THE MAKINGS OF
A FAMOUS FOOTBALLER

CHAPTER TWO

I was trimming Castro's dad as we drank rum and black on the rocks. Squeaks bounced after a while and left me, Castro and his dad there chilling. Merv crossed my mind. I knew what he was like, so I dialed him in to see wha gwan. He was wondering where us man were but he didn't have no credit. He had linked some chicks he wanted to bring us in on. We told him 'bring them yes!' There was only two though and three man, but man said, 'don't watch nutten, its cool'. About half an hour later, Merv was on the endz. This time he had outdone himself. Both of them were smooth. Yasmin was smoother, but Charlot was decent too. Charlot was for me on the night, straight off the bat, Yasmin was feeling Castro. The only problem was, Merv was on her. He done already said he was on Yasmin. Castro didn't care though. After we chilled together for a while, I took Charlot to my yard, Castro took Yasmin into his and Merv went home pissed.

Me and Charlot done a ting but she never let me beat. It was all good though. It was a nice evening. The next day, Merv come asking questions. I told him everything, giggling, but he weren't feeling Castro's stories and now Castro and Yasmin were dealing (going out). It was a disrespect stealing Merv's chick in the first place, them being family and that. But now, man's dealing with her too. The funny thing was, she reminded me of Jasmine in a lot of ways - it was a Tottenham ting. They didn't know each other, but they lived two minutes from each other. But at the same time, she had nothing to do with me, so I didn't care. Castro didn't need me telling him nothing anyway, his game was tight. Remember! Merv knew, karma would find Castro though. He just left Castro to Yasmin and wished them the worst. (The worst soon come!)

BACK ON ROAD

CHAPTER THREE

Justin from red head days had been out of jail a few weeks all now, but I hadn't seen him yet. He had formed a group in there and he was getting publicity with Xcons. Imagine man dem from the ends, fresh out of jail shaking hands with Prince Charles. Getting interviews with the Sun and BBC. That shit was big! Justin was The Links Man all now. He was rolling with Bigga, Rustie and Terra and it looked like they were going on with tings when they got Party in the Park. Man in London were wishing them the best tru we all remembered the MOBOs - when Method and Red Man came and disrespected the spot. We loved them man, but if the establishment had let the man dem in, them man would have had some respect. They kicked over chairs, smoked weed inside, stood on tables and I remember Beverly Knight saying, "if anyone's going to be in here doing this, it might as well be London man." It was the fucking truth and now Justin's in Xcon's I felt like next time the MOBOs came, it was gonna be us man up inside acting up. We all deserved it and why shouldn't it be us? I wanted to see him, I had plans and I hadn't seen him in jail tru he didn't know where I was so he couldn't send me a VO.

I was fucking with this chick from Nottingham name Gemma at the time. She actually looked a little like Jasmine, back off was crazy too but a bad attitude. She was like Jasmine in too many ways - but she was what I needed to understand Jasmine could be replaced.

I hadn't seen Mumsy for about a year all now and she must have been missing me cause she told my brother to tell me to come home. I remember my brother dropping me to the door, waiting for Mumsy to open - then leaving. Our home was broken, there was no togetherness in my family. Mumsy stood there at the door for a minute looking at me in shock. It's like she expected to see a crack head standing there in front of her. When she let me in we talked and she asked me about Jasmine. I told her, 'I'm not seeing her again.' I could see she was happy about that. She didn't know what I had been through or how close she was to being a permanent member of our family but I didn't tell her.

TO BE CONTINUED

Similar Genre and Associate Authors

Von Mozar: Ignorance Kills

Von Mozar: Sexfiend

Von Mozar: Little Jamaica

Von Mozar: Mr Bling

Levi P.S: Through My Eyes (The Spirit Of A Prince)

Robyn Travis: Prisoner to the Streets

Sherlock: Different, Different Part 2

Jonathan Buffong & Brenda Downes: Warriors of the Cage

Jasmine Johnson: Mr Soon Come

Chrisitian Niova Diawara Small: Wake up and smell the Fufu

Courttia Newland: The Scholar (A West Side Story)

Jaja Soze: Street Boys

Ted Pitman: The Monkey Bars of Life

Pearson Nurse: My Journey through Racism

Bernie Grant MP: Dawn to Dusk

Claudine Duberry: Guns, Gangs & the Implications for Social Workers

Further Education

AFRICAN HISTORY

Llaila O Afrika: African Holistic Health

Llaila O Afrika: Melanin

Robin Walker: When We Ruled

Ivan Van Sertima: They Came Before Columbus

David Muhammad: Black Studies

Chancellor Williams: The Destruction of Black Civilization.

CC Blackman: Towards the Destruction of a Nigger Mentality

Robin Walker: Blacks and Religion (Volume One)

Walter Rodney: How Europe Underdeveloped Africa

GOOD BOOKS

Jose Silva: The Silva Mind Control Method

David Morehouse: Remote Viewing

Charles Arthur: The Art of Passing the Buck

Richard Edwards & Nigel Stockwell: Trusts and Equity

Robert Kiyosaki: Rich Dad Poor Dad

Nathalie Nahai: Webs of Influence

Malcolm Gladwell: The Tipping Point

Organisations Helping the Community

www.ukblack-links.com
www.accessuk.org
www.reachsociety.com
www.father2father.com
www.robertlevyfoundation.org
www.jimmyasherfoundation.org
www.communitiesfirst.uk.com
www.afreshstartct.org
Family Circle Consultancy